Sarada Ramakrishna Vivekananda
Associations of Oregon,
San Francisco,
& Hawaii

JNANA MATRA
THE WISDOM PARTICLE

by *Babaji Bob Kindler*

©2014 Babaji Bob Kindler
All rights reserved.
Published by SRV Associations

No part of this book may be reproduced in any manner without written permission of the author or publisher except for quotations embodied in articles or reviews. For further information write to:
SRV Associations
P.O. Box 1364
Honoka'a, Hawaii 96727
srvinfo@srv.org   www.srv.org
             or
SRV Hawaii
P.O. Box 380
Paauilo, HI 96776 USA

The publication of this book was made possible by donations from friends and students of the SRV Associations.

Printed in the United States of America

ISBN 978-1-891893-16-2
Printed in the United States of America

Acknowledgement

Our thanks to Rama Nand Tiwari of Pilgrim's Books for the use of many of the images in this book.

Contents

Introduction ix

Chapter One — The Wisdom Word And Its Many Facets 1

Chapter Two — The Impenetrable Cell Wall of the Jnana Matra . . 49

Chapter Three — The Essential Triputi and "The Fourth" 70

Chapter Four — Stream of Consciousness and Turiyatita 84

Sanskrit Glossary 93

List of Illustrations/Charts

Jnana Matra, Atom of Wisdom 5
The Sevenfold Road to Ruination 11
Pratibha — The Power of Intelligence 13
The Six Treasures and Six Divine Powers of God 15
The Nine Limbs of Bhakti According to Sri Ram 19
Fundamental Facts About the Mantra 26
Vedantic Secrets of the Scriptures 31
Echelons of Fire 39
Trividham Duhkham — The Threefold Sorrows of Existence 47
The Palette of Conscious Future Lives 53
Prakasha Shakti — The Revealing Power. 57
Some Obstacles and Solutions in Spiritual Life 63
The Three Matras of AUM in the Mandukyopanisad 73
The Four States of Consciousness & Seven Attributes of Turiya . . . 75
The Three Stages of Indian Philosophy 79
The Fourteen Stages of Upper and Lower Knowledge. 81
Jnana Matra, Atom of Wisdom (repeat) 85
Lokas, Nadis, and the Transmigration of Souls 87

Dedication

To those true teachers of the Dharma,
who both recognize and transmit
the Wisdom Yoga
that is so crucial and indispensible
to gaining Liberation
in this very life.

Introduction

Like billions of dew drops glistening in the early morning sunlight, all reflecting the light of the one sun, just so do countless souls inhabiting a myriad worlds all shine with the scintillating Light of Spiritual Awareness called *Atman*. This is all made possible by the emanation of infinite wisdom particles that radiate from The Word, *AUM,* and thereafter congeal into gradated strata of consciousness-filled realms as they trickle down from station to station via levels of intensity of vibration.

If even one of these particles were split, similar to splitting an atomic particle of matter, the result would be an implosion of intelligent Light that is the very nature of revelation. Unlike an external atomic explosion, however, with its host of destructive properties and possibilities that darken the world and create mass karma, the implosion of an intelligent particle shreds the curtain of *Maya* and illumines the cosmos at all levels of its manifestation, thereby conferring positive benefit on all living beings.

Intelligent particles without number, called *Jnana Matras* by the ancient seers of Mother India, form an ocean of Bliss, *Ananda,* that is the singular possession of the luminaries of different religious traditions. It is these bits of living Awareness that hum, like millions of tiny bees imbibing nectar inside a massive Lotus, giving The Word its "Soundless Sound." The sacred songs of India proclaim that the yogis meditate in dark mountain caves so as to catch the sacred and primal pulsation of this sagacious sea of orotund sound, which transforms and transports both their minds and their meditations.

On earth, these very particles are at the foundation of everything that has taken form. Atoms, molecules, protons, neutrons, quarks, and subatomic particles are only the outer material expression of the underlying flow of streams of these incredible increments of pure Intelligence. Even objects beheld by the imperfect senses are really only solidified thought, or concretized intelligence, though hosts of beings — materialists, sensualists, intellectuals, scientists — see them otherwise.

Where some see mere matter, then, and others see *maya*, and still others see only a mystery, the wise see Mother — Mother Wisdom. The Divine Mother presides over this infinite ocean of potential, sending intelligence forth in waves and drawing it back in eternally. The physical world, with its oceans, rivers, and streams, is just an external model for the many tributaries that are constantly flowing to and from the Ocean of pure, conscious Awareness, called *Brahman*. *Shakti*, Its dynamic power of ebb and flow, takes particles of Its essence and fashions them into worlds and beings. These She takes back, as well, after their play is over, only to send them forth to sport again in cycles.

To see the Ocean of Consciousness, then, is to become aware of its waves and particles. At the physical level this is the realm of Quantum Physics, but at the spiritual level this is called the Yoga of Meditation leading to samadhi. The first set of initial samadhis are of wisdom, called *savitarka* and *nirvitarka* by the yogis. They are followed by *savichara* and *nirvichara*. Basically, all four consist of beholding the entire Ocean of Wisdom within oneself. Since this vision is accompanied by powerful waves of bliss *(sananda)*, a necessary period of overwhelm is the usual result. This is also called *"jada"* samadhi, or a stunned state. Beings like Christ and Lord Buddha experienced this samadhi. When we hear of the inwardly rapt mental condition of Jesus Christ in the wilderness, or of Lord Buddha under the Bodhi tree, we can better understand what jada samadhi is like. But when the initial shock of this realization has died down, the seer of such a rare spiritual state sees that this Ocean is comprised of millions of bits or cells of Consciousness. He also finds out that these can be seized, as it were, and brought close for internal inspection. This is where meditation, the seventh limb of Lord Patanjali's Yoga, turns into samadhi, the eighth limb.

From here on in, meditation proper will never be the same for the seer again, that is, no effort or vaunted aspiration need ever attend his efforts thereafter. The "Goal" sought after has been reached, and all that is left is to imbibe, digest, and joyfully ride streams of particles inward to any destination desired or preferred. Even the total dissolution of all sense of individual separation into the Ocean of Consciousness — the highest Samadhi — is now possible. As one great luminary once expressed it: *"Have no hope for me forever more. I am gone, and gone forever!"*

These few introductory paragraphs on the exceedingly wondrous theme of the intelligent particle, *Jnana Matra*, must suffice to usher the reader and, hopefully, the aspirant, into the realm of oceanic Awareness — an oceanography of an entirely different and unique nature. For, plumbing the depths of the boundless Ocean of timeless, deathless Awareness is given to only a few, and they must be intrepid inward wayfarers indeed.

As a sort of underwater map of endless regions, then, the following chapters will light on and explain — as far as words can express — what awaits the divine diver after precious gems, who also seeks the Pearl of Great Price in the depths of the Sea of *Satchidananda*. May those who attempt to immerse themselves in such nondual bliss never lose track of the streams of living Consciousness that take one across the sea of this world and beyond all sufferings. As the Upanisads state: *"Omityevam dhyatha atmanam svasti vaha paraya tamasah parastat — Meditate upon the Self as AUM, and Godspeed to you in crossing over to the farthest shore beyond all darkness."*

Chapter One

The Wisdom Word And Its Many Facets

The testament of John concerning The Word — *"In the beginning was the Word, and the Word was with God, and the Word was God"* — is well known, even to the materialistic western people of this day and time. Thousands of years earlier than Christianity, however, the Vedic seers who enunciated the *Rig Veda*, the world's oldest scripture, expressed it this way:

> *"Then Nonbeing was not, nor Being. What was that ocean impenetrable? Then death was not, nor immortality. 'That' was one, and lived independent of the breath by its own Permanence. There was nothing else beyond or other than It.*
>
> *Darkness concealed in darkness in the beginning was all this Ocean of Existence. When chaos atomic covered It, then That which is ever One appeared by the power of Its own energy.*
>
> *Who knows of this? Who here can declare it, whence this creation was born, and whence was the loosing forth of all beings. The gods know not; they only exist below by the force of the creation; who then can tell from whence It originated?*

Whence this creation came into being, whether He established it or had no hand in it, He who regards it from above, in the Supreme Ether, only He knows — or perhaps He knows not."

In addition to all the wisdom teachings that such an ancient scripture offers up, there is also the amazing fact of how far advanced in the art of spirituality were these seers of Mother India, living at least 5000 years prior to the Christian era.

Other traditions, springing up later, were no less interested in The Word and its "beginning." The Chinese, both of the Confucian and the Taoist persuasion, being deeply influenced by the auspicious advent of Buddhism from India, also expressed their thoughts on it. Huai-nan Tse wrote, *"That which was before all individual existences, and which was without action although capable of action, is That which preceded heaven and earth."* As Chuang Tse put it later, and more simply: *"Essence without form divided Itself; then a movement took place and life was produced."*

In a more recent and much more poetic expression, the famed Sufi mystic, Jalal-uddin Rumi, stated: *"I looked on High and I beheld in all the spaces, That which is One; below, in all the foam of the waves, That which is One; I looked into the heart, it was a sea, a space for worlds peopled with thousands of dreams: I saw in all the dreams That which is One."*

This "sea" that the luminaries have beheld, and which they have tried their best to describe throughout time, is the subject of this small book, a tiny offering to the thoroughly divine nature of its content. That superconscious consistency is herein being explained in terms of billions of inherently intelligent particles that this Sempiternal Sea possesses as Its very core Essence. Everything that partakes of Wisdom, higher and lower, and that speaks of or intimates Knowledge of any type, like *Paravidya* and *Aparavidya* to the ancient seers of India, is the property of this ecstatic and eternal Ocean of Awareness. Anyone who values the above mentioned qualities will naturally be a devoted adherent to all that It contains, provides, represents, and emanates.

There are precious few words in English, and in European language in general, that can provide adequate descriptions for axioms and principles that are purely spiritual in nature. The word, "emanation" is a good English example, carrying with it an almost breathless sense of beatific expression. The Word, as an ultracosmic principle *(Mahatattva),* virtually radiates with pure intelligence, which is really as close to Pure Awareness as the mind can go without losing itself, as Shankara says, *"like a hailstone in an ocean."*

The aftereffect of the advent of intelligence, in terms of emanation, formulates subtle realms *(lokas)* of name *(nama)* and form *(rupa)* in time *(kala)* and space *(desha).* These four words — nama, rupa, kala, and desha — form a fitting way to express both the appearance of lifeforms on various worlds, as well as to explain the host of phenomena that follow, that are themselves, aftereffects of their own design. In fact, the word, "effect" *(nimitta),* brings in its train the entire field of action and the karma that is always and ever associated with it.

Intelligence as knowledge is the finest and foremost of all effects, being the cause of everything that falls below The Word. As the world teacher, Swami Vivekananda puts it: *"Though Knowledge, being a compound, cannot be the Absolute Itself, it is the nearest approach to It, and higher than will or desire."* This explains that part of John's statement, *"....and The Word was with God...."* It is via intelligence that beings rejoin their Essence, Pure Awareness, after they have sported in the worlds of name and form in time and space that all consist of *Jnana Matras* — Wisdom Particles.

Our first and main chart for this book, displayed on the facing page, takes The Word apart and reveals Its inner and outer workings — particularly with regard to the embodied soul, the *Jivatman*. For, the knower of The Word is able to sport in consciousness with form free of any of the lasting effects of taking on the five sheaths of ego, intellect, mind, energy *(prana)*, and body. These five are coverings over Reality, and are necessary overlays that the Jivatman assumes in order to separate itself out from the Ocean of Pure Awareness, rather like five jars of lesser to greater size, filled with water and placed inside of one another and capped off. As Lord Vasishtha states in his scripture, *Yoga Vasishtha:* *"Ego, plus mind, plus intelligence — and adding in the five senses — make up this temporal unit called the psycho-physical being. When considering it and its powers, we must remember that when these eight facets are kept in a pure state, then She, the Kundalini Shakti, loves to sport in this amazing form."*

Keeping these facets of embodied divinity *"in a pure state"* is, as most practitioners of the *dharma*

ॐ Jnana Matra — Atom of Wisdom ॐ

"The bodies of beings which appear in the form of a framework of bones and sinews, is the self of the nature of food. Further within, is the self of Prana, split into five. Deeper still is the self of the nature of mind, different than these. Even deeper than it is the self of the nature of intelligence. At the deepest of all distinct levels is the self of the nature of Bliss....."

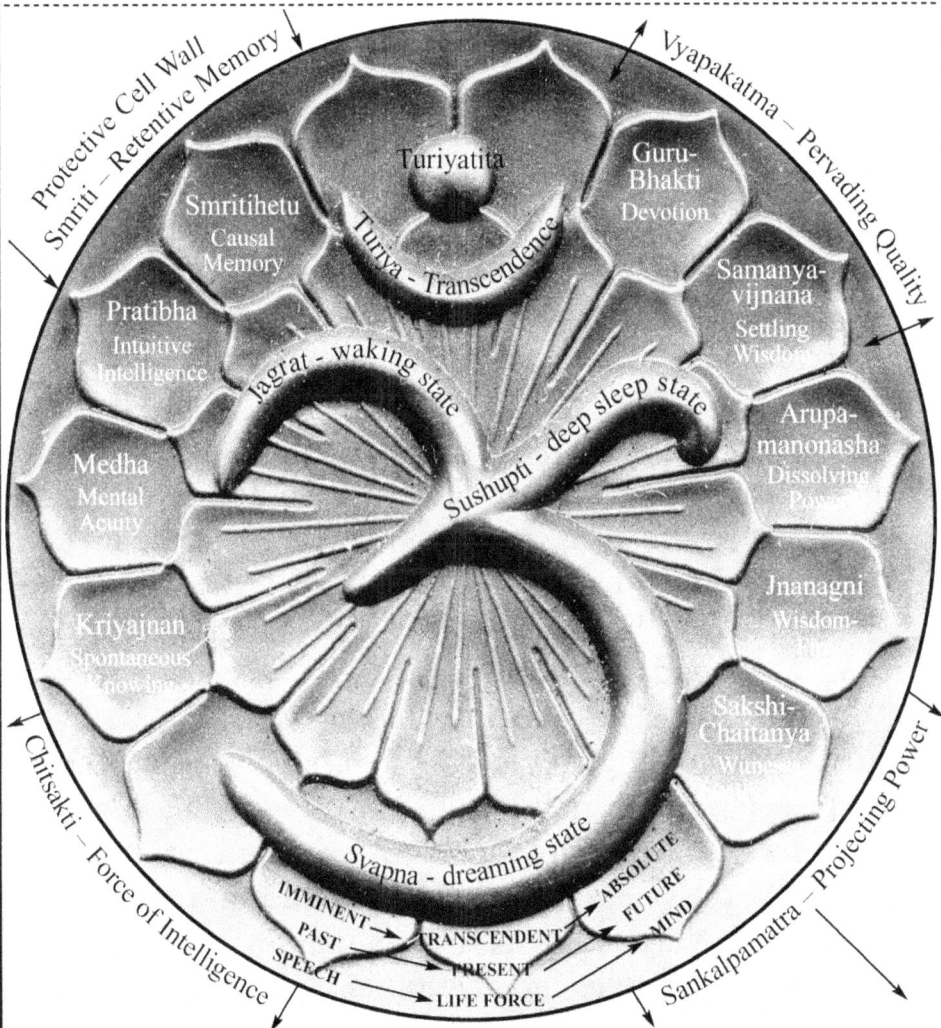

"....food is pervaded by vital energy; vital energy is pervaded by mind; mind is pervaded by intelligence, and that ever happy intelligence is pervaded by Bliss. This self of Bliss is pervaded by Brahman, the Witness, the innermost of all. Brahman is not pervaded by anything else. Neither by action, nor by begetting children, nor by anything else, only by knowing Brahman, does one attain Brahman."
                                                                            Katharudra Upanisad

Chart by Babaji Bob Kindler   Property of SRV Associations

know, not an easy task. Millions of souls presently on earth and in the body have both failed in this task, and lost memory of the art of divine life that was clearly demonstrated by beings such as Lord Buddha, Jesus Christ, Patanjali, Vedavyasa, Shankara, Chaitanya, and others. Nor are most even interested in regaining this now obscure art, being content with matter, senses, objects, pleasures and, unfortunately, the negative side-effects of an unwise preoccupation with all of these. Content to suffer, they may develop a weird type of forbearance in order to continue their enjoyments, but they throw away in turn the unalloyed bliss of Pure Consciousness and its many exceptional fruits in the offing.

While on the subject of the Five Sheaths, the quote in two parts, placed at the top and bottom of the chart now under study (page 5), relates classic Vedanta. The first, and outermost sheath, is called *annamayakosha*, which literally means that covering that is formed of food. *Annam* is translated as matter, or food. The Sanskrit root, *anu*, translates as atom, a tiny particle. According to the *Katharudra Upanisad*, this sheath is pervaded by the *pranamayakosha*, the sheath of life-force, filled with particles of *prana*. That is pervaded by the *manomayakosha*, the sheath of mind, which sports particles of mentation that form thoughts. The sheath of intelligence (*jnanamayakosha*) pervades mind and the other two, while the sheath of bliss, called *anandamayakosha*, pervades all of them. To put it succinctly, *"....food is pervaded by vital energy; vital energy is pervaded by mind; mind is pervaded by intelligence, and that ever happy intelligence is pervaded by Bliss. This self of Bliss is pervaded by Brahman, the Witness, the innermost of all. Brahman is not pervaded by anything else. Neither by action, nor by begetting children, nor by anything else — only by knowing Brahman — does one attain Brahman."*

By this quote we not only come to see the layers of consciousness associating with form, but how fine the principle of intelligence is. The only thing finer in the realms of name and form is to be a knower of the bliss of pure Intelligence. When the meditator focuses on the ocean of wisdom, he/she finds an infinite supply of wisdom particles and feels unimaginably blissful. This is the first level of samadhi *(savitarka/nirvitarka)* according to the Father of Yoga, Lord Patanjali. The next level *(savichara/nirvichara)* consists of taking these living particles, one by one, and examining them inwardly to gain all-pervasive insight.

Petals of the Inmost Lotus

Examining the subtle Jnana Matra, the Particle of Intelligence, we see it on the chart (page 5) as being represented by the many petals of a lotus. Each petal expands eternally and is ever nourished by The Word, AUM, which is the Sanskrit symbol inscribed in the lotus.

The first petal to be scrutinized, on the upper left hand side of the chart, is titled **Smritihetu.** Even as a concept only, the idea is an engaging one. The translation in English is "causal memory," which for the novice implies remembrance of something that happened early on in life, like in the womb.

But *smritihetu* is memory in the human mind of

the inception of all worlds and all beings, stretching back through the internal Life Heavens and the regions of the Deities to the primal vibration of The Word, and filled with that bliss, *Ananda,* just referred to above. In other words, every soul has in its distant recall the memory of the bliss of samadhi and the Oneness of Divine Reality, called *Brahman.* Beings who are considered enlightened are just souls who have reclaimed samadhi via spiritual practices like meditation, and now live in full awareness of their divine nature, *Atman.*

What to speak of the cognizance of bliss inherent in the mind's memory, all of the experiences that the soul had over the unending course of its lifetimes are also stored there. Examination of these in meditation is illumining, to say the least. In successive stages of meditation, examining past lifetimes is an important facet of spiritual practice. By doing so the awakening soul not only discovers the mechanics of conscious embodiment, and notes the Witness of the process (his/her own Self), but finally understands all the traits, qualities, karmas, and impediments that are within. This is why the *Svetasvataropanisad* states in its early chapters, *"Practicing the art of meditation, the ancient seers beheld the Divine Being (devatmashakti) in everything, which though veiled by its own projected forms of nature, was nevertheless one and indivisible, and which had been incomprehensible to them earlier due to the limitations of their own intellects."*

The quality of *smriti,* memory, needs more explanation here. As the requisite of *shruti,* hearing the revealed scriptures in the Vedanta, as the *niyama* of *svadhyaya,* study and memorization of slokas and sutras in Yoga, and as *astika* in Tantra, devotion to the spoken and the written word — all of these and more will require a firm and facile memory. The youth of ancient India were taught to sit in yogic posture early on in childhood, and listen to the spiritual preceptor discourse on the truths of the dharma. Raised in spiritual wisdom, the problems of life that would have otherwise attended the soul as it attempted to make its way on earth, simply expired early on, leaving the young aspirant with the time and energy to contemplate the Way and attain the Goal — the Way being the spiritual path, and the Goal being Enlightenment.

Along the Way leading to the Goal, then, the aspiring soul only has to sit quietly whenever problems and impediments rise up in life, and access that treasurehouse of profound solutions stored up in the vault of smriti. For deeper answers concerning problems of a subtle spiritual nature, such a soul will resort to deeper meditation. At that level, smritihetu, if it is accessible and kept uppermost in memory, will come forth and settle all such matters. The spiritual wayfarer only needs to make sure that worldliness in the form of various distractions is avoided, keeping the mind fresh and resilient.

The word, "retentive," comes into prominence here, for long term memory of what one hears in the present life eventually develops into the ability to remember valuable teachings in future lifetimes. It is no coincidence, nor is it a special blessing from God, that some embodied souls are born with wisdom, while others have to work hard to acquire it. If the truth be known, the only real blessing from God in this context is the actual presence of Wisdom existing as Intelligent Particles — *Jnanamatras.* The embodied soul only has to find a way to access them and put them into service of that selfsame God abiding in mankind. Smriti, retentive memory, and smritihetu, causal memory, show the way.

If these two facets of original wisdom are blocked by ignorance, forgetfulness, and the like, then no abiding knowledge that is really worth having ever presents itself to the embodied being. The veils that fall over divine remembrance are formed by distractions such as pleasure-seeking, attachment, hoarding and coveting wealth, greed, and selfishness. The fruits of these are flagging vital energy, failed health, depression, loss of self-worth, and ensuing suffering of all sorts. The chart on the facing page, a teaching from Lord Krishna in the *Bhagavad Gita,* reads the riot act on this darksome side of life. The chart needs no running commentary, and is placed here merely as a reference, for the enrapt reader of these pages.

Returning to our main chart on page 5, we take up the next petal of the Jnanamatra, called **Pratibha,** Intuitive Intelligence. In the earliest ages, around the time of Lord Vasishtha and Sri Ramchandra, in the middle period at the time of Vedavyasa and the written Vedanta, and later in the time of the Eight-limbed Yoga of Lord Patanjali, this word held slightly different meanings. But all of them pointed to one salient fact — that of inherent wisdom that precedes matter.

In the present age and time, Sri Ramakrishna Paramahamsa has indicated pratibha to be a *"flint-like intelligence"* that remains resilient even in an age of

● The Sevenfold Road to Ruination ●
The Mayic Map of the Brahman Bypass

"Brooding on sense objects, man develops attachment to them; from attachment comes desire; from desire anger sprouts forth. From anger proceeds delusion; from delusion, confused memory; from confused memory the ruin of reason; and due to the ruin of reason he perishes." Sri Krishna, Ch. 2, B. Gita

"Mental imbalance threatens yogic equipoise and meditation. Through practice of japa and spiritual exercises the mind ceases to react and becomes impervious to brooding and depression, and the unsteady emotional states they cause."
Lord Patanjali

Broodway Blvd.
Worry Way
Lust Lane
Attachment Avenue
Oversight Overpass
Stress Street
Error Expressway
Desire Drive
Passion Place
Anger Alley
Fear Freeway
Travesty Terrace
Delusion Detour
Chaos Circle
Confusion Court →
Ruination Road

"That one who is overcome by attachment, which creates entanglements in this world, his sorrows duly increase like bamboo grass in the rainy season."
Lord Buddha

"One cannot completely get rid of passions like lust and anger. Thus, one must direct them towards God. For instance, if desire comes, transform it into yearning for realization of God. In the case of lust, that impulse must be turned into the desire for intercourse with the Atman. With anger, feel angry at all that stands in the way towards realizing God."
Sri Ramakrishna

"Loss of one's memory is caused by the mind's constant acts of misidentifying the Self with the nonself. Focus on the Self and give up the distractions of worldly talk and music, desire-based thoughts, and the like, and affirm your oneness with Atman." Sri Shankara

"Absence of discriminative wisdom, want of mastery over the senses, and the inability to stem desires and egotism in the mind — these three culminate over time in delusion which in turn results in mental diseases that settle in the mind like snow on the ground in winter. Mental delusion results in the performance of negative acts which then form karma and give rise to physical diseases." Lord Vasishtha

"Ruined souls of small intellects and fierce deeds, bewildered by fanciful desires and enmeshed in the snare of delusion, they fall into a foul hell. These unfortunates get hurled into the wombs of the demonic and deluded and, reborn again and again, then fall into a condition which is lower still." Sri Krishna

Chart by Babaji Bob Kindler
Property of SRV Associations

darkness, like the Kali Yuga. The metaphor utilized for it is that of a piece of flint that immediately strikes sparks even after lying in a riverbed for centuries. Even while it is still wet, if struck against a stone, it will emit fire. Of course, the Great Master had as His disciples beings like Swamis Vivekananda and Brahmananda, who were the most excellent examples of flint-like intelligence. Even as young boys, Naren and Rakhal were on fire with the spirit of divine intensity.

To explain more adequately, and to make connections within the periphery of the wisdom particle and its subtle content, it is a great attainment for the soul to have access to retentive memory, but an even more wondrous feat to be able to not only recall spiritual truths, but to put them into action as well. The many ways in which pratibha gets utilized stand as a prime example to this force of positive manifestation. At its best, and when used by a past master, it is spontaneous and lightning swift. The chart on the facing page illustrates some of its powers and uses.

The philosophy of pratibha, as revealed on the new chart just opposite, is based in four connected principles. First, there is the principle of *pratibhasikasatta*, the cosmic dream projection. Usually designated as the sportive play of the Trinity — *Brahma, Vishnu,* and *Siva* — it is the appearance of name and form in time and space based in duality and multiplicity — put more simply, *Maya*. Crores of souls embody in order to play in the realms of manifested consciousness, which as we are studying, is really an immersion in the ocean of intelligent particles, though few here on earth see it that way.

Pratibha — Power of Intelligence

"Everything — the world, manifestations therein, enjoying, suffering, and departing, and the power of conjuring the realms of name and form, can and should be directly designated and attributed to one's own intelligence. Other factors such as fate, destiny, karma, and even grace, also reside within and spring from that selfsame power." Babaji Bob Kindler

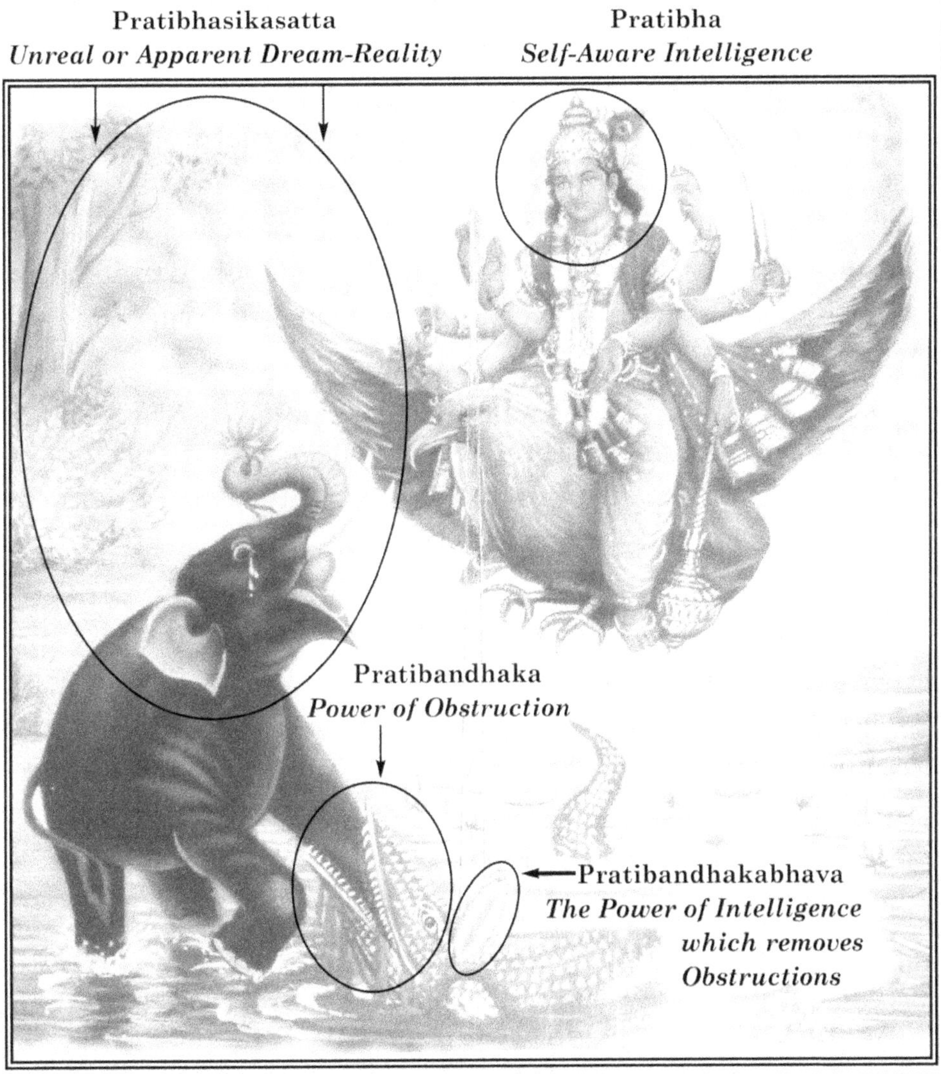

Pratibhasikasatta
Unreal or Apparent Dream-Reality
Pratibha
Self-Aware Intelligence
Pratibandhaka
Power of Obstruction
Pratibandhakabhava
The Power of Intelligence which removes Obstructions

"Gods and goddesses, father and mother, or any other kith or kin, cannot confer greater benefit than that of the well-directed intelligence. This intelligence is incomprehensible and exceedingly subtle. It wanders wherever and whenever it desires. Therefore, the wise ones carefully watch over this intelligence, which resides in the cavern of the heart, and utilize it to free themselves from the shackles of Mara." Lord Buddha

Chart by Babaji Bob Kindler

Secondly, there is present the power of obstruction, *pratibandhaka*. On the cosmic level, this is the doing of the projection itself, often and misleadingly called "creationism." But on the collective and individual levels where embodied souls are concerned, it includes the mind and its penchant for covering or veiling — like covering the Truth with all manner of overlays, for instance. The elephant in the picture represents the soul caught in the binding power of its own false superimposition. It may wander about for awhile in an ocean of happy preoccupation, but left bereft of pratibha — its own power of revelation — it will come to suffering and grief before too long.

Herein enters the final two facets of *pratibha* and *pratibandhakabhava*. Pratibha, as the wisdom particle (see chart on page 5) reveals, is the intuitive element itself that, when called up by the human will and brought to the fore of thinking consciousness, will always save the soul sporting in relativity. Its manifestation is the very power of intelligence. As the chart on page 13 illustrates, it is like the grace coming from on High, from the Supreme Soul. The quote on the bottom of the chart by Lord Buddha explains well the inherent power each soul has available within the principle of its own innate intelligence.

The petal in the wisdom particle that represents mental acuity, called **Medha,** comes up next for scrutiny. In Vedic philosophy, Mind and its Intelligence are two of the Six Divine Powers of God, (see chart on facing page) along with Love, Knowledge, the Universe, and the Jiva — the embodied soul. That God (*Ishvara*, God with Form) utilizes all of these preternatural principles as powers and transforms them into much more

The Six Treasures and Six Divine Powers of God

"As the web comes out of a spider, and sparks come out of fire, so this whole universe proceeds from the Beloved Goddess, the Primal Force of Existence. We salute Her, the Mahashakti, within whose mayic power this whole universe, moving and unmoving, is projected, sustained, and withdrawn." <u>Vedavyasa</u>

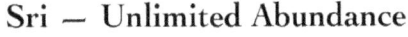

Sri — Unlimited Abundance

Bala — Magnificent Glory

Aishvarya — Irresistible Strength

Vijnana — Penetrating Wisdom

Tyaga — Natural Renunciation

Tejas — Awesome Splendor

Chart by Babaji Bob Kindler   Property of SRV Associations

The Six Divine Powers of God

Jivatman — Living Beings
"The jiva at first remains in a state of ignorance. He is not conscious of God, but of multiplicity. Then he becomes conscious that God dwells in all beings."

Jagad — Universe
"This universe is God's glory. People see His glory and forget everything else. They do not seek God. This universe has evolved from the Supreme Brahman."

Manas — Mind
"Regardless of the path one follows, yoga is not possible until the mind is stilled. The mind of a yogi is under his control; he is not under the control of his mind."

Buddhi — Intelligence
"A man's intelligence is very delicate and can get covered, distorted, or misled. He must therefore practice many austerities so as to acquire Divine Knowledge."

Prema — Love
"What is Prema? The one who feels It, this intense and ecstatic Love for God, not only forgets the world, but also forgets even the body, which is so dear to all."

Jnana — Knowledge
"Intelligence, devotion, compassion, renunciation — these belong to the realm of true knowledge. With these a man comes near God. One more step and he attains God."

than they seem to be, or are assigned credit for by human beings.

Thus, mental acuity is precious, and needs to be recognized, acknowledged, and put to work for the manifestation of God in human form who is expressing Itself on this earth. The chart on page 15 demonstrates how the Rishis of India have always seen the human form and its sportive play *"As God walking around on two legs,"* as Swami Vivekananda has stated.

One of the teachings around the ability called Medha has to do with blending it with the heart. *Medhakendra,* then, is the result — the intelligence of the devout heart. As Swami Vivekananda has stated, the devotion of the heart devoid of discriminative wisdom risks becoming surface-like and sentimental, while the knowledge of the intellect lacking communion with the heart tends towards dryness and sterility. Thus, a happy marriage of these two chief facets of the human being is advised. If both meditation and selfless service are added into this marriage, like two dharmic and obedient children, then there is nothing in life that cannot be attained and rightly utilized for Divine Life.

Kriyajnan is the last petal on the bottom left hand side of the main chart under scrutiny on page 5. The Sanskrit word, *"kriya,"* is a potentially problematic one in present times, much like words such as *siddhi, karma, guru,* and others. Deep study in the tradition is necessary before the aspirant can make real sense out of such loaded words, and use them in the proper way. In the case of the word "kriya," it has many meanings, ranging from action, to breathing exercises in hatha yoga, to more esoteric expressions in Tantra. Particular yogas have also been named after it, the more current ones in present times aligning their teachings with sensationalism, mystery-mongering, occult powers, and preoccupation with the psychic level of existence.

The very best of Kriya Yoga, however, is found in the authentic *Ashtanga Yoga* of Lord Patanjali. In it, he merely selects the three best of all preliminary disciplines in spiritual life — austerity, study of scripture, and devotion to God (*tapas, svadhyaya,* and *ishvara-pranidhana*) and coalesces them into an effective system for making sure progress along the spiritual path. This he terms Kriya Yoga — the Yoga of austere practices. Here is where the truest and best meaning of the word kriya comes forth, and when it is mated with the word "jnana," indicating that superlative spiritual wisdom that destroys ignorance, a force for swift and immediate enlightenment is unleashed. Applying it towards spiritual attainment, the seeker is able *"....to become a yogi is six months,"* as Swami Vivekananda has said.

And it is not a falsely hoped for shortcut to samadhi that the great soul is referring to here, but the coming of age of the seeker after Truth based upon steady sadhana leading to direct spiritual experience. For, swiftness of thinking is a quality that not many embodied souls are blessed with, but rather, that some few earnest practitioners are born with. That is, they have been pursuing it, and other special qualities, for lifetimes. Attributes of such high standing are not bestowed by grace and divine dispensation, but are earned via dedication and determination. At the level of salvation, some boons are conferred, but in the realm of liberation such ground is hard won. Kriyajnan is part of this ground of spiritual emancipation. One sees it only in those who have duly reached a lofty pinnacle of illumination, such as authentic teachers of the dharma.

Moving to the right in our inspection of the Jnana Matra, or Wisdom Particle, the moist petal of **Guru Bhakti** presents itself for consideration. The word "intelligence" implies love for the Divine Reality it embodies. For, we know what we love, and we love what we know. The two — love and wisdom, devotion and knowledge — are virtually the same.

And nowhere are the two more perfectly conjoined than in the spiritual teacher, the Guru. A manifestation of love and wisdom on earth, the Guru is a preceptor of dharma and a past master at interpreting and transmitting the truths of the scriptures. This is partly because such a unique soul knows that everything that is connected with The Word is full of pure, living, sentiency. Just as atomic particles flow in streams, so too do Atmic particles, their Source, do the same. More will be said about this in coming chapters.

To give an idea of how bhakti infuses the Wisdom Particle, and temporarily departing from the main chart on page 5, the chart on the facing page is offered. In it, each limb of devotion is a representation of wisdom flow.

In the <u>First</u> <u>Limb</u>, transformative intelligence is coursing from guru to shishya via wisdom transmission that gets facilitated by wise occupation with Holy Company. Intelligence is in the teacher, in the words he is speaking, in the scriptures he is quoting, and importantly, in the ethers that are vibrating with streams of wisdom particles that cannot be seen. But

The Nine Limbs of Bhakti According to Sri Ram

"Association with the holy ones, reciting accounts about the Lord, singing God's glories, hearing and transmitting God's teachings, devout service of the teacher, sense-control and ceremonial worship, repetition and contemplation of the Lord's mantra, seeing God in all beings after attaining nonattachment, and investigating the true nature of Brahman — these are the Nine Limbs of true and authentic Bhakti."
Sri Ramachandra

Association with the Holy
"Through the company of the holy arises nonattachment; through nonattachment arises freedom from delusion; through freedom from delusion arises steadfastness; through steadfastness comes liberation."   *Shankara*

Spreading the Teachings
"They who are well-grounded in knowledge, and who share their wisdom, who rejoice in freedom, full of light, they win nirvana even in this world."   *Lord Buddha*

Singing God's Glories
"What purpose can these ears serve if every sound is not heard as the sweet nectar of God's Names, flooding our eyes with tears of ecstasy?"   *Ramprasad*

Hearing the Teachings
"You will find Me in those sacred places where My Names are being chanted and My teachings are being transmitted."   *Sri Krishna*

Serving the Teacher
"Whoever is devoted to God, and delights in service of the teacher, to such a person Moksha is an attainment already at hand."   *Sri Ram*

Undergoing Purification
"If but one fiber is sticking out, it will be impossible to thread the needle. Likewise, if purification is not practiced early on, realization will not be possible."   *Sri Ramakrishna*

Reciting the Mantra "Gain control of the life-force in a natural way. Through the practice of japam and meditation you will reach the stage of kumbhaka without risking the dangers which may easily come from the practice of asana and breathing exercises."   *Swami Brahmananda*

Seeing God in All "God is the act of giving; God is the offering; and by the Lord is the offering given into the Lord for consumption. The highest state of consciousness is gained by those who see the Lord present in everything."   *Bhagavad Gita*

Realizing Brahman "The scattering form of the mind is activity which manifests as pleasure and pain. The darkening form is dullness that tends towards injury. The gathering form is the struggle to focus. The one-pointed form is the tendency to concentrate, and the concentrated form is what brings us to samadhi."   *Vivekananda*

Chart by Babaji Bob Kindler   Property of SRV Associations

their effects are seen in the aspirant who, paying close attention, is changing for the better minute by minute via the sounds he is hearing and the connections they are making.

In the Second Limb, that selfsame stream of wisdom particles that the gracious guru radiates in wisdom rays upon the disciple can now be turned in another direction so as to benefit all those who are ready and qualified to hear it. Though of less intensity when coming from the student, who is only "sharing" the teachings and not consciously transmitting them as of yet, the innate potency for opening hearts and changing thinking patterns is nevertheless present. The dedicated aspirant thus passes on the teachings humbly, to the extent that he or she comprehends them. By sharing the dharma with others, more knowledge and experience come forth.

The Third Limb of Bhakti is directly infused with wisdom particles, manifesting as the essence of tone, the flow of sublime melody, suggestions of related harmony, and the presence of engaging rhythm — all in conjunction with the profound meaning of the slokas, chants, lyrics, mantras, and bijams that are utilized. All of this gets expressed in the purifying emanation of the heart's devotion. Sacred stotrams, bhajans, gazals, and other reverential musical offerings of Mother India are not mere sweet devotional songs; they are devotional wisdom songs.

In India's ancient and timeless forms of music there are no mundane messages, no superficial lyrics, no sentimental deviations, and no insipid worldliness. Everything present there is specifically about God, for

God, and with God. For the one engaging in this holy pastime, devotion and wisdom merge, leading to a naturally inward state of spontaneous meditation on Reality. These three main Yogas — *bhakti, jnanam*, and *dhyanam*, can lead nowhere else but into service of God in mankind (karma yoga) as a matter of course.

Thus, the Fourth Limb of Bhakti, called *shruti* and *shravana,* hearing the teachings of the dharma, is a natural follow up to the third limb. In fact, many of the scriptures are actually sung in Indian tradition. Many are named songs, *gita*. It is as if to melt the heart, galvanize the mind, and overwhelm the human ego, that teachings and music are placed together in one form. Even when music is not directly utilized, as in lecture, discourse, and wisdom transmission, words, well delivered, are still considered melodious and tuneful. Their convincing cadences, coming in streams of wisdom particles, disenchant the mundane mind from its preoccupation with mayic thoughts and cause it to dance in newfound freedom. As Swami Vivekananda states in one of his devotional wisdom poems: *"Foaming flow cascades — a streaming music — to which echo mountain caves in return; warblers, full of sweet-flowing melody, hidden in leaves, pour hearts out — love discourse."*

The sources of these "love discourses" are no less connected to the lofty phenomena of wisdom particles. Gurus, who are preceptors of scriptural and spiritual knowledge mentioned in the fifth limb of bhakti within our sub-chart presently under study (page 19), embody the Jnana Matra. Not only have their minds, thoughts, and intellects been given to it completely, but even their physical body has been sacrificed in order to make use of it. As Swami Vivekananda states, again, *"This has been taking place through eternity, that one builds a bridge by laying down his own body and thousands of others cross the river through its help. It is only the great saint who can work, making a mountain out of an atom of virtue in others and cherishing no desire but that of the good of the world."* The word "atom" here speaks all the more towards the hidden secret of particles in everything. Man only has to look beyond the physical particle, which has been an amazing discovery on its own merit, and take the clue from it and begin to search for the source of his thoughts. Whereas outer observation combined with scientific advancements will suffice for the former, the consummate seeker will have to utilize inward meditation for the latter.

Along this line, the content of this famous Vedantic limb needs little explanation. Suffice to say, that to hear the truth *(shruti)* is not enough. The seeker must contemplate It *(shravana)* to uncover all essential particles — beyond both outer and inner meanings.

<u>Limb</u> <u>Five</u> of the *Nine Limbs of Bhakti* also speaks of the principle of service, called *Mahat Seva* in ages long past. Besides being a key facet of the Nine Limbs, service of the guru is also one of the Four Sentinels taught by Lord Vasishtha. Thus, it occupies an honorary position in the minds of the spiritual. In the Bhagavad Gita, Sri Krishna states:

tad viddhi pranipatena paripashyena sevaya
upadekshanti te jnana jnaninas tattva darshinah
"The qualified student approaches the wise teacher via humility, service, and cogent questioning. Then that wise one initiates him into the highest Wisdom."

Thus is service of the teacher advised by sacred scripture, and recommended by authentic luminaries. In recent times, Sri Ramakrishna Paramahamsa utilized many stories about the guru in order to let people know that they need to take an adept guide for spiritual life: *"Once, a novice interested in medicine tried to learn how to check the pulse of people, practicing on his friends, but was unable to make any progress. He then approached one friend who was a doctor, and in all humility asked to keep his company. By doing this he swiftly acquired the progress he was seeking."*

Swami Vivekananda has made copious references to the Karma Yoga, service of God in mankind, giving it a new breath of life in this day and time. In the spirit of devout service he coined phrases such as *"work as worship,"* and *"labor as love,"* to prompt living beings to fulfill this important limb of devotion. To give an idea of how deep and serious is the devotion for the guru in India, the following excerpt from a devotional song by Swami Vivekananda is presented.

"I make a complete offering of myself to my Guru, who is an all-powerful wave of purity rising out of the ocean of shakti. Whose lila floods the being with a love that destroys all doubts, and who is the ultimate healer of the chronic disease of worldliness and attachment.

"I surrender my life, mind, and soul to the Divine Lord who appeared in human form, and whose superhuman actions are inconceivable to mortals. Whose life reveals and exemplifies nondual Truth, and removes the incapacitating effects of relative existence."

The Sixth Limb of Bhakti has to do with purification of the mind, senses, and body — preferably in that order. *Chit Shuddhi*, purification of the aspirant's thoughts, duly leads to the highest qualification for Enlightenment. As Sri Ramakrishna Paramahamsa has stated, *"Pure Mind is God,"* falling in direct concurrence with Lord Buddha's affirmation that *"Pure Mind is Buddha Mind."*

With such a unique sterling mechanism as this, the many problems encountered with the five senses, their objects, and the body, are easily overcome, whereas trying to purify the body and senses first often takes too much time. Further, in the time that it takes to effect the aforementioned purification, many sidetracks and deviations can arise to spoil the progress of spiritual aspirants, and even take them away from the path. Swami Vivekananda defines both the goal and the problems of this matter in his own inimitable way:

"In the world, all things are done by people guided like lifeless machines. There is no mental activity, no unfoldment of the heart, no vibration of life, no flux of hope; there is no strong stimulation of the will, no experience of keen pleasure, nor the contact of intense sorrow; there is no stir of inventive genius, no desire for novelty, no appreciation of new things. Clouds never pass from this mind, the radiant picture of the morning sun never charms this heart. It never even occurs to the mind if there is any better state than this; where it does, it cannot convince; in the event of conviction, effort is lacking; and even where there is effort, lack of enthusiasm kills it out."

With mind in order, i.e., possessing such powers as proper perspective, right attitude — all the elements of Lord Buddha's Astangika Marga, for instance — the senses and the body will follow like trained puppies. Like five white horses, perfectly disciplined to be and pull together under the single will of the charioteer, the five senses will lead the seeker after higher wisdom and deeper devotion towards the ultimate Goal of full Enlightenment. Because, after all, we hear the phrase, "enlightened mind" all the time; we seldom hear, "enlightened senses" or "enlightened body." Mind lends sentiency to everything, but only when it aligns itself with Pure Sentiency of the Soul, Atman.

<u>The Seventh Limb of Bhakti</u> is all about mantra practice and its efficacy. Mantras, which are many — all correlated to the diverse deities that populate the inner subtle worlds of Consciousness — are shared almost equally by Jnana, Raja, and Karma Yogas. These sacred statements, attended by their seed syllables *(bijams)*, are to be recited in Jnanam (knowledge of what they mean), in Raja (during meditation and formal sitting practice), and in Karma (noting how divine recitation effects everyday life and activities).

To cite a famous teaching, the initiate should actively engage in mantra recitation knowing what each word and its *matras* (letters/particles) signify, and to which deity the mantra connects within. All of this is to be watered daily by the tears of devotion for God in the form of the *Ishtam,* the Chosen Ideal. Without that deep feeling for God in form — "in form," where beings suffer the most — there can be little growth or fruition in these other crucial modes of practice. As Sri Ramakrishna has stated, *"A man cries jugs of tears for matters relating to family, friends, and occupation, but he cannot cry even one tear for God. If he could, he would immediately experience a taste and sense of freedom."*

In order to deepen our knowledge of ancient

Fundamental Facts About The Mantra

"God cannot be realized through japa, worship, and meditation. God is only realized through His Grace. Nonetheless, one must perform japa and meditation, for they can remove the impurities of one's mind. God's Grace then becomes revealed." — Sri Sarada Devi

Is the Science of Cosmic Sound
"Through the science of mantra the Kundalini will awaken. Repetition of God's name will lead to the goal."

Is Vedic in Origin
"The rishis of ancient Vedic times practiced mantra and other austerities to realize God."

Is Unique among Spiritual Practices
"Such is the power of the mantra that, in addition to the mind, it also purifies the body."

Is a Universal Mode of Practice
"People in other countries are also repeating recitation of the Lord's Holy Names."

Is Effective as Repetition
"Even if your mind does not awaken, you must repeat the mantra thousands of times."

Originates in the Bodhi Mind
"After attaining true wisdom one sees that gods and deities are all Maya."

Grants Knowledge of Unity
"Man achieves the highest goal through the practice of japa. God has given us fingers that we might be blessed by repeating His Name. Be content under all circumstances and repeat His Name."

Provides Protection during Practice
"God's name protects. Instead of losing a leg, one might merely suffer a thorn of the foot."

Clears the Subconscious Mind
"Man becomes pure and the mind still, by repeating the mantra of God."

1/4 of the Mantra is given by the Guru at time of Initiation
"The true purpose of initiation is to try to realize God through sincere effort."

3/4 of the Mantra is Hidden as Mother's Form
"When a pure soul repeats the mantra, the holy name bubbles up from within."

Mantras are Associated with Deities and are Innumerable
"The Master gave me mantras possessing great power, all of them associated with the deities. They are imbued with the power of renunciation."

Chart by Babaji Bob Kindler

Property of SRV Associations

mantra science, the chart on page 26 gives a dozen crucial facts surrounding it, all accompanied by quotes from The Divine Mother, Sri Sarada Devi, who perfected it in this age and then utilized it to help others. Through this we can see that the practice of mantra is simple, but qualification to receive it in sacred initiation, called *Mantra Diksha,* is comprehensive. It should not be merely taken from a book, a friend, or a misguided soul of self-assumed status. It has to be given by a spiritual teacher *(Guru)* who has had it directly transmitted by a luminary who has received it from a long-standing lineage versed in mantra science. Then only is it truly effective.

One of the great benefits of mantra is its simplicity. It is in this absence of complexity that the mind finds its rest, not only free of the many modes of mentation that the mind is always subject to, but free of the many waves of thought that continually wander across the surface of the mental field. The mantra has been likened to a tidal wave that consumes all other waves in its sweeping approach, leaving only one major principle to contemplate — that of the Ishtam.

<u>The Eighth Limb of Bhakti</u>, "Seeing God in Everything" is, according to Sri Ramakrishna Paramahamsa, the final step of spiritual realization in this world, in this body. The famous words, *"I will wait,"* uttered by the young Sarat (later, Swami Saradananda) to his guru, Sri Ramakrishna, when he was told he could not yet receive that boon, echo in the collective mind of contemporary Vedantists everywhere in this day and time.

The apparent contradiction in this statement is

one that, when contemplated, reveals the subtle nature of philosophy and its methods, especially with regards to Mother India. Vedanta states that the world is unreal, and only God is Real *(brahman satya jagad mithya)*. This is gleaned from practice and realization of the *neti neti* ("not this, not this") form of sadhana. When neti neti has been realized, however, i.e., that objects, worlds, pleasures, and such can never satisfy or satiate the human soul, the more advanced practitioner realizes the "God is Real" portion of the aforementioned great statement and attains *iti, iti* — "all this, all this." It is then that he/she perceives Consciousness pervading everything, everyone, and has to conclude by affirming "All this is Brahman." That is Seeing God in Everything.

This deepest insight of authentic spiritual life cannot be feigned; it is not a matter of lip service offered glibly and prematurely by beings who are still attached to pleasure and attended by worldliness. The mind, senses, and body — as shown under the heading of the Sixth Limb of Bhakti — must be purified before such a statement can carry the weight of Self-realization measured by direct spiritual experience. More about this spiritual summit will be discussed in other portions of this book concerned with the *Jnana Matra* — The Wisdom Particle.

The Ninth Limb of Bhakti indicates Realization of Brahman, Divine Reality. It also indicates that all levels of mind previously held by the soul have been transcended, one by one, resulting in that rare condition the seers of India call Nonduality, or *Advaita*. Consciousness is one and indivisible, but it occupies many different stations. This occupation of bodies and vehicles occurs through subtlety or density of vibration and capacity. Generally speaking, it is a matter of association when its host is subtle, but a matter of identification when the host is gross. This distinction, in turn, is applicable due to intelligence, i.e., the Wisdom Particle. If vibrating Consciousness identifies with water, for instance, then the body formulated will be a fish or aquatic creature. If the senses of hearing and smelling become predominant, a dog's body is formed.

This science of vibration and identification of Consciousness is most subtle when it comes to human beings. The manner in which awareness assumes forms reflects an inner nature whose past experiences in other bodies come into play. Here, in the human context, if Consciousness identifies with the unrefined and uncontrolled human ego, the result is a brutish human being, capable of committing all manner of atrocities. If Consciousness descends and associates more with the refined human ego, there appears the intellectual person whose mind is able to reason and perform acts of altruism, etc. Finally, and most marvelous, it is when Consciousness associates with the pure and fully spiritualized human mind that a seer, sage, or saint appears.

These beings, few and far between on earth, live in the nondual Awareness that is the essence of full-blown realization in the human form. This state, if it could be called such, is indescribable, and so has to be experienced for oneself. It is a matter of revelation that the Nine Limbs of Bhakti all head for and are inclusive of the formlessness of Nondual Reality, Brahman.

The Nine Limbs of Bhakti, illustrated by the

chart on page 19, has been explained to further elucidate one of the precious petals of the Jnana Matra — *Guru-bhakti* — from our main chart shown on page 5.

Moving on with our in-depth exploration of that chart and the essential elements of its wisdom particle, we encounter the petal of **Samanya-vijnana.** It occupies a very subtle increment of the *Jnana Matra*. Though utilized as far back as the ancient times of Lord Vasishtha, it is a prime entry in Sanskrit dictionaries of the time, its many descriptions ranging in the form of everything from "homogenous intelligence" to Brahman Itself. Interestingly enough, if the word *"samanya"* is taken by itself and defined, it means "simple" or "ordinary." The implication, then, is that pure, conscious Awareness is most natural, a principle that is simultaneously obvious and subtle. This describes both the intelligent particle and those who have awakened to the wisdom stream it belongs to as it courses through the awakened minds of luminaries past and present.

Partaking of the wisdom particle is a matter of envisioning it and identifying it. *"Yesterday's imagination is today's visualization, and today's visualization is tomorrow's realization."* Principles unseen, and previously unknown, are what spiritual life is all about, especially at the outset. What is possible once the *Jnana Matra* is realized beggars the imagination.

Revelation of scripture, for instance, proceeds from utilizing these imperceptible intelligent particles. *Vijnana* refers to the highest form of Wisdom. To give an example of how much is contained in an infinitesimal increment of wisdom principle, the following chart is displayed for examination, explanation, and study:

Truth is as clear as a bell. Wisdom is as familiar

Vedantic Secrets of the Scriptures

"Those virtuous ones alone gain moksha who, from their early childhood, train themselves in Atmajnan scriptures in the company of holy beings. Therefore know, oh sedulous seeker, that the state of Brahman is attained via the combination of the illumined preceptor, the jnana-shastras, and the sincere disciple." — Lord Vasishtha

The Three Great Sources
Vidya-Shastra – Consulting the Revealed Scriptures
Guru-Anushashana – Instructions from a Preceptor
Aparokshanubhuti – Verification by one's own Experience

Three Techniques of Interpreting Scripture
Prati-tantra Siddhanta – as Separate Doctrines
Sarva-tantra Siddhanta – by Way of Reconciliation
Sahaja-tantra Siddhanta – by Way of Natural Synthesis

The Two Types of Knowledge
Paravidya – Spiritual and Revelatory
Aparavidya – Religious, Secular, and Intellectual

The Four Views on the Origin of Scripture
Apaurasheya – Of Divine/Eternal Origin
Ishvariya – Originating from Ishvara
Archa – Originating from the Seers
Paurasheya – Originating from Human Intellect

Three Potent Practices
Shravana – Listening
Manana – Contemplating
Nididhyasana – Realizing

Three Proofs of Truth
Shruti – Hearing Truth
Yukti – Reasoning Truth
Anubhava – Experiencing Truth

"Atmajnan scriptures treat Self-knowledge and lead to Divine Wisdom. Ordinary shastras treat terrestrial knowledge and lead to further bondage. But even the Atmajnan scriptures will be nonproductive if the imp of lower mind attached to conventional and secular knowledge is not exorcised thoroughly." — Lord Vasishtha

Chart by Babaji Bob Kindler — Property of SRV Associations

to the soul as breathing is to the body. The Light of Consciousness is immediate revelation. Philosophy, though amazingly comprehensive, is nevertheless a matter of pure reason. Jnana Matras, Wisdom Particles, make it all so.

In the chart on the previous page are seen several secrets to the longevity and transforming power of the Indian schools of Philosophy, called *Darshanas*. The Sanskrit word "darshana" means "to clearly see." All paths that are authentic, and imbued with real wisdom, i.e., charged up intelligent particles, can cause the soul to directly perceive facets of Divine Reality. Debate and argumentation are hardly the point. The Holy Mother, Sri Sarada Devi, stated: *"Is Divine Reality, Brahman, a subject for argumentation or common discussion, like the bartering for fish and greens in the marketplace?"* In brief, Brahman can never be described, but It can be inferred, and philosophy — when it is at its best and most succinct — is the superior mode for doing so.

The intelligent particle reveals the secret of *shruti*, *yukti*, and *anubhava* — or *shravana*, *manana*, and *nididhyasana*, as described cogently in the Vedanta school *(Uttara Mimamsa)*. These two *triputis* are seen at the bottom of the chart on page 31. Shruti/shravana means to hear. The unawakened soul needs to hear the words of Truth abiding in the revealed scriptures from the mouths of illumined souls in order for spirituality to take the fore. *Jnana Matras* permeate the threefold order of this process, i.e., the truths of the scriptures, the listener, and the one speaking the truths. The successful passing on of the Truth from teacher to disciple is called a "wisdom transmission."

Once this preliminary act has been accomplished, the disciple takes what he/she has heard and engages in *yukti/manana*. Inside the mind (manas) of the listener, a revolution is taking place, and if close attention is paid to this divine upheaval in the form of concentrated effort, the meanings heretofore hidden in words, *slokas, sutras, mantras, mahavakyas*, etc., get mentally digested and settle in as mature wisdom. Now all that is left for the disciple to do is to realize the results of such contemplation, *anubhava/nididhyasana*, and bring them into life for the highest good of all beings.

This completes the necessary process of sacred study. The intelligent particles — previously lying under the surface of human consciousness with all its weights and worries — are now charged up and streaming along newly forged subtle passageways, *"nadis."*

One of the beautiful results of the stream of intelligent particles along these fresh pathways is the sense of freedom that accompanies it. The mind is released from old habits and modes of thinking as the light of intelligence cuts its way through the gloomy areas where such darkness dwelled for so long. Old *samskaras* — grooves worn into the mind's makeup due to repetitive thoughts and acts — are smoothed over, and new impressions are created. The divine life that sets in more than justifies all that has gone before in the form of suffering, striving, effort, study, and the like.

Effective intelligent particles both contain and reveal. We must remember, looking back on other facets of the *Jnana Matra*, like *smritihetu*, causal memory (refer to chart on page 5), that it is all a matter of subtle mnemonics. Human intelligence, like pristine underground rivers, is always flowing under the surface of superficial, habitual, and conventional mind. To those who do not wish to awaken spiritually, these reservoirs of living Consciousness will remain submerged and untapped. Though present and therefore accessible, the potential for higher wisdom, *vijnana*, which is indigenous, even common, *samanya*, to the human mind, will remain a mystery. Thus, one fair and fragrant petal of the Intelligent Particle will be left undiscovered. This is much more of a misfortune than all the sufferings and recurring karmas in the world, since all of these would get dissolved in that mellifluous flow of streaming Intelligent Particles that make up the substratum of all of Existence.

Continuing on with the latest chart on page 31, we are shown more of higher wisdom in all its subtlety. There, the Three Great Sources, namely *Vidyashastra*, *Guruanushashana*, and *Aparokshanubhuti* — stand as testaments to the presence of the *Jnana Matra*. That is, it takes far more than luck, good fortune, or serendipity to create a thirst for the revealed scriptures, discover a wisdom teacher, and gain direct spiritual experience — all in one lifetime. Those beings who have helped the petal of *Samanya-vijnana* to blossom in a previous lifetime will have a great advantage here, as recognition and recall, dwelling in the mind at the behest of the Wisdom Particle, open the way.

These beings will also possess preternatural intuition around the four types of origins of scriptural wisdom (*paurasheya, archa, ishvariya, apaurasheya*), the difference between secular knowledge (*aparavidya*) and spiritual knowledge (*paravidya*), and the ability to interpret the teachings of the scriptures as well. In beings unavailed of natural wisdom, however, the recondite triple steps of Philosophy — dualism, qualified nondualism, and nondualism (see page 79) — will remain mixed together indiscriminately in the human mind. As is the case with a major percentage of the human population in this day and time, they will not think to avail themselves of the precious teachings of the dharma and the way to imbibe and realize them.

    The teachings referred to herein, that are a main ingredient of the *Samanya-vijnana* aspect of the Jnana Matra, have a deep relationship with balance and equilibrium. The knowledge there is "settling wisdom," for it ushers in qualities like contentment, peace, and equanimity of mind. *"You need peace of mind first and foremost,"* spake the Holy Mother, for at this stage of existence, called a human being, it is the mind that will usher one into the presence of the Atman, the eternal Soul.

    But the destruction of ignorance is the price of admission, and nothing does away with the superimposition of ignorance like knowledge. The *Jnana Matra* contains special subtle petals that bring about the demise of root ignorance and all its evolutes. The main chart on page 5 shows them up as *Arupa-manonasha*, dissolving power, and *Jnanagni*, wisdom fire.

    Arupa-manonasha is the powerful acid of Truth that proves to the embodied soul that its real nature is formless. That is, once all gross and subtle forms of ignorance have been disintegrated by various types of insight via self-effort, *sadhana,* the final barrier of root ignorance, *mula-avidya,* must expire as well. Swami

Vivekananda tells of this singular process that moves from the dual to the nondual via stages, arriving at last at the pinnacle of realization called moksha, or mukti: *"I will compare Truth to a corrosive substance of infinite power. It burns its way in wherever it falls — in soft substance at once, hard granite slowly, but it must."*

The "soft" substances mentioned here are the grosser forms of ignorance that are common to most beings who have not yet espied the unusual characteristics of Consciousness — the unique facets of human Awareness that are unparalleled in all of existence. The Six Passions (lust, anger, greed, delusion, vanity, and jealousy), the Eight Fetters (hatred, shame, lineage, pride, fear, secrecy, caste, and grief), the Four Deadly Traps (guilt, sadness, depression, low self-esteem), the Three Enemies of Reason (egotism, intolerance, and narrowness), and the Three Stupefactions (worldliness, insensitivity, and jadedness) are some of these; they should never be allowed to intrude upon the sacred land of human life and dharmic doings. There are also the effects of all the above as well, that form the many weights of consciousness that descend due to reactive emotional states that complicate the picture. These swiftly vacate the thinking process when knowledge, wisdom, and Truth are adhered to.

The corrosive acid of Nondual Truth will penetrate and dissolve all the above easily in a short period of time. What may take longer to do away with are the abiding wisps of ignorance that persist at the causal level of the mind. These are unseen phantoms of the mind such as past karmas *(sanchita),* and the hidden impressions *(samskaras)* that riddle and partition the subconscious and unconscious mind. Also, the presence of the three *gunas* which, though encountered and subjected to finer and finer measures and methods, like meditation, still insinuate themselves on the soul's bid for the nondual state.

But the advanced spiritual aspirant, or the adept, has one powerful element in his/her favor at this most precarious level of the inner process: it is forward motion, natural momentum. The Wisdom Particle has gathered great impetus over the soul's journey of awakening, and a simple matter of proper application at the most auspicious time works wonders in favor of the intrepid practitioner who will settle for nothing less than full Enlightenment. Suffice to say, it is no wonder that reliance upon this beneficial thrust is the spiritual mead of the luminary.

Along the subtle trajectory of achieving the nondual state, the soul gains the helpful faculty to formulate and dissolve, in turns. Tellingly, most beings neither know about nor seek the rare ability of dissolution. Attachment to matter, objects, and pleasures in them dictates otherwise. It is only when impediments such as doubt and fear are removed from the quotient that the soul can experiment with doing away with all forms — even the sense of individuality, or ego, that persists into the later stages of spiritual attainment.

The power of dissolution, then, found in the Wisdom Particle's facet called *arupa-manonasha,* has many uses, to be sure. But its real boon is its facility of taking away the mind and its thoughts, ideations, and conceptions. As the Father of Yoga, Lord Patanjali, has stated: *"Yoga, union with Divine Reality, is brought about by the cessation of the mind's thought waves."* As any long-term meditator knows, the most difficult thing in meditation, in day by day practice, is rendering the mind void of all vibrations. Objects may be cast away fairly easily as one sits to plumb the depths of Consciousness in meditation, but thoughts of objects persist tenaciously.

And this is where the next petal of the lotus of the *Jnana Matra* applies (page 5). **Jnanagni** is the sentient Fire of Wisdom that burns unceasingly at the heart of the Wisdom Particle. Sacred Fire plays an important role in every Wisdom Tradition of the world, and the Vedic religion is no exception. In fact, nowhere is the real essence, meaning, and purpose of fire so well expressed than in India — certainly not spiritually. The chart on the facing page (39) reveals the state of this Inner Fire in gradated stages, or echelons.

Noting the bottom half of the chart, the teaching has it that fire is in everything, and everywhere. As this relates to mankind, however, is the most important thing. That is, fire as a matter of idol worship, or comfort, or for its own sake, etc., is incomplete in its scope. The practical is okay, but the purificatory and the mystical are far better.

In the diagram at the right is seen a graph showing the gradated levels of fire's influence. The Fire of Suffering occurs early on, for unlike its companion, happiness, the miseries of life can be helpmates towards the goal of transcendence, or even to the maturation of forbearance at the earlier stages. In fact, the presence of suffering often drives the soul to more noble pursuits, which is why the fire of aspiration follows.

◄O► Echelons of Fire ◄O►

⸱ The Significance of Fire in Vedic Religion and Philosophy ⸱

"First harnessing the mind and the senses with a view to realize the Truth, and then having found out the meaning to the light of Fire, the evolving soul brought itself out of the earth."

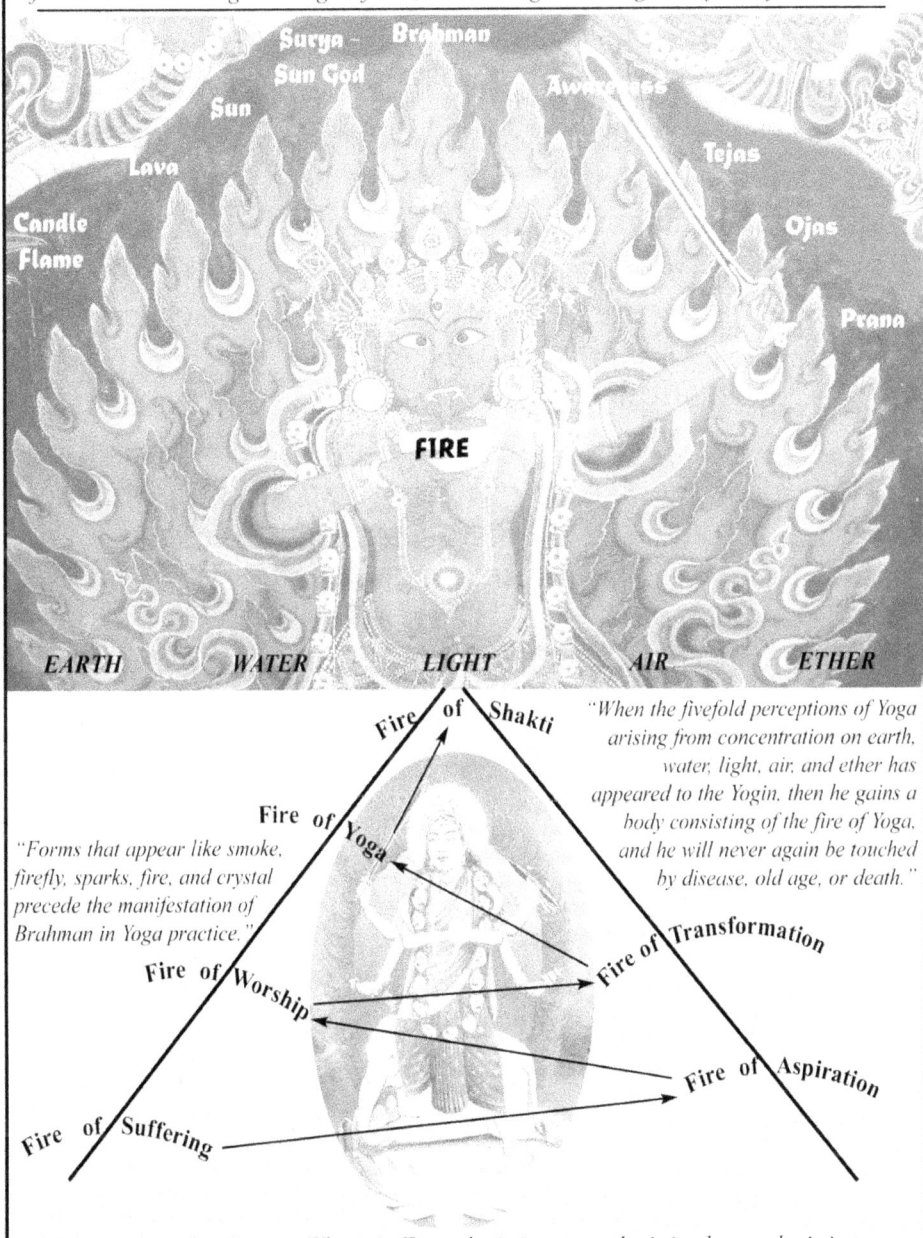

Labels on upper image: Surya – Sun God, Brahman, Sun, Awareness, Lava, Tejas, Candle Flame, Ojas, Prana, **FIRE**

EARTH — WATER — LIGHT — AIR — ETHER

Fire of Shakti
Fire of Yoga
Fire of Worship
Fire of Transformation
Fire of Suffering
Fire of Aspiration

"Forms that appear like smoke, firefly, sparks, fire, and crystal precede the manifestation of Brahman in Yoga practice."

"When the fivefold perceptions of Yoga arising from concentration on earth, water, light, air, and ether has appeared to the Yogin, then he gains a body consisting of the fire of Yoga, and he will never again be touched by disease, old age, or death."

"Salutations to that Divinity Who is in Fire, who is in water, who is in plants, who is in trees, and who has pervaded the entire universe."

Chart by Babaji Bob Kindler   Property of SRV Associates

It is this tendency towards aspiration, sometimes referred to as yearning, that opens the gates for bonfires yet to burn. The one that ignites in the "hearth of the heart," called the Fire of Worship, is one such. In many of the Nine Limbs of Bhakti just covered in the earlier part of this chapter, it is the Fire of Worship declared there that sets the stage for the meeting of God with mankind. It also sets the conventional world aflame to facilitate that. For, worship is accompanied by the heat of purification. In the *Bhagavad Gita*, for instance, Sri Krishna declares that the best austerity of the body is worship, like puja.

But worship, and the transformation that takes place partly due to it, are two different levels of fire. Therefore, the Fire of Transformation ushers in an entirely new level of yogic heat, cutting the soul with the "Diamond Blade" of Intelligence in the image of the Spirit. This is the irrepressible Fire of Yoga. In Swami Vivekananda words, he states: *"Our Bengal is a land of bhakti and jnana, where yoga is scarcely so much as talked of. What little there is, is but the queer breathing exercises of the hatha-yoga — which is nothing but a kind of gymnastics. In the mountains I feel very well, and all without taking any medicine. It is exercise that promotes health, not medicines, and the 'Fire of Yoga.' Sitting up on the snow peaks of the Himalayas, I repeat from the Upanisads: 'He has neither disease, nor decay, nor death, for verily, he has obtained a body full of the Fire of Yoga.' Thus I am very well, and all without taking medicine, only by the exercise of mental healing."*

The only fire left after the Fire of Yoga is the Fire of Shakti. In the context of the Wisdom Particle, the only difference between these two forms of fire is one of subtle degree. The former is real intelligence, and the latter is Dynamic Consciousness Itself.

The upper half of the chart on page 39 gives a "flame by flame" gradation of fire in its many modes. The "Mind Only" schools of Indian philosophy take their name from the assertion of the seers that the universe we see outside of us was neither evolved over millions of years, nor created in seven days. Put very simply, its origin is not in time, but in thought, for time is really just a thought, i.e., a concept in the mind. Further, the universe is not a location in space, either, but a territory, or *loka*, in Consciousness.

Following this way of perception, all of the millions of suns burning in the nocturnal skies are thoughts, or projections of mind at its cosmic, collective, and individual levels. They may as well be atoms, i.e., particles of a greater whole, in their own right. And just see what kind of power they possess!

The gradated levels of fire shown on the chart (page 39) can be best understood using this subtler mode of perception. From candle, to lava, to the sun, and on inwards to the god of the sun, *Surya, "one Light shines."*

And this is where the Particle of Intelligence, *Jnana Matra*, reveals its secret. That one Light of Intelligence is indivisible, to be sure; everything shines with Its radiance alone. It is only a matter of intensity of expression taken together with the capacity of any given vehicle. In other words, how much of intelligence can any given body — physical, heavenly, causal, spiritual — receive and retain?

Another way to explain and understand this revelation is via the science of vibration. But if vibration to one level of scientist means atomic, material only, and what is Atmic, imbued with Supreme Intelligence, is left out of the equation, then no final conclusion about Reality can ever be drawn. The human mind will be left with only relativity. Though the finite occupies the Infinite, the latter will be overlooked and only the finite will prevail.

But what about the deep insights of the Seers of Reality? In the Upanisads is stated: *"There, in the innermost Consciousness of every living being, the sun shines not, nor the moon, nor stars, nor fire, nor lightning — much less this tiny mortal flame. That One Light shining, all else shines. By Its Light all is made luminous. May that one Light of pure, conscious Awareness enter into us and permeate us to the very core of our being."*

On the far right hand side of the upper half of the chart on page 39 are seen levels of gradation concerning another aspect or mode of Sacred Fire. This has more to do with subtle forms of energy rather than physical, heavenly, and spiritual bodies. *Prana*, vital energy running through the elements, objects, bodies, and minds, is most definitely a form of fire.

In the *Bhagavad Gita* there exists a much utilized sloka that is recited aloud as a blessing over food to sanctify it before conscious consumption. That is:

Brahmarpanam brahmahavir brahmagnau bramanahutam bramaiva tena gantavyam brahmakarma samadhina.

The overall meaning has to do with the presence of Divine Reality, *Brahman,* in everything, even in the very food that we eat. That is *brahmagnau,* the fire of Awareness that consumes all things. For, and in the body, the food offered there is a type of fire, as in "vital energy." The fire of our ability to act brings it to the mouth and into the stomach, where the fire of digestion takes over and breaks down physical matter, turning its subtle remains into life force.

That life force, prana — shown in the chart under study — has gross and subtle forms to it. As *mukhya prana* it promotes and signals good health. As prana, proper, it circulates the blood, supplies the organs with nutrition, causes the lungs to inhale and exhale, and even carries thoughts inward and outward — from the first world of physical matter, to the second world of mind and mentation. In the third world, as in deep sleep, it ceases to flow — like in the suspended breath, and most functions are reduced to stillness and inactivity. As the Upanisads say about the human soul at that time, *"The hawk sleeps in its nest."*

But subtler directions are being tracked as well. The ordinary soul, unawakened as of yet, may traverse the three worlds all of the time, but he/she does so unawares. When *prana* turns to *Ojas* (refer to chart on page 39) due to the aspirant's practice of sadhana, subtle energy in sanctified food is getting further refined, and the result will be the exuding of light from the radiant mind — even from the pores of the physical frame. In the Yoga Sutras of Patanjali, the Father of Yoga states: *"The refined body of the yogi possesses beauty, strength, firmness of thought and activity, and is able to forbear any troubles which may afflict it."* In this way is the Fire of Yoga accomplishing its singular and salutary work.

Ojas, the refined force of intensified comprehension, signals another stage, one that facilitates the transmission of dharmic teachings to others. The wondrous fire that accomplishes this is called *Tejas*. This Sanskrit word is defined in dictionaries as "spiritual brilliancy," "the element of fire," "the heat of austerity," and several secondary meanings as well. Suffice to say that the seers describe it as the ability to transmit high quality teachings of a subtle nature to certain highly qualified students who are ready and capable of understanding them.

This specialized fire is also associated often with the awakening, rise, and habitation of Kundalini Shakti amidst and within the six *Satchakras* leading to arrival at the crown, or the *Sahasrara*. For more on this esoteric and essential system, the reader may refer to the recent book, *Reclaiming Kundalini Yoga*, by the same and present author.

Returning to the chart on page 5 to take up another petal of the *Jnana Matra*, or Wisdom Particle, we find it titled **Sakshi-Chaitanya.** Both of these Sanskrit words are filled with subtle implication and power, the former indicating the presence of a transcendent Witness of all beings, relationships, objects, and phenomena, and the latter pointing us to our true divine nature as pure, conscious Awareness. Thus, the Wisdom Particle contains within it an essential modicum of Nondual Reality, much like the precious human being sports the Divine Spark of *Atman*. Thus, it is the Wisdom Particle that both cognizes and fuels the cosmic process, particularly the jiva's (embodied being's) important part in it.

In the Upanisads and other nondual scriptures of Mother India, the Witness, *Sakshi,* is described as *"....the self-luminous observer of all beings and phenomena in relativity."* Also, *"....the cognizer of the presence and absence of knower, knowledge, and what is knowable."* The famous sloka regarding it is:

Brahmanandam paramasukhadam kevalam jnana murtim dvandvaititam gagana sadrisham tattvama sadilaksham ekam nityam vimalamachalam sarvadhi sakshi bhutam bhavatitam trigunarahitam sadgurum tam namami

"We salute the Leader of our souls through whose grace our ignorance is dispelled, who is beyond good and bad, pleasure and pain, life and death, and all other pairs of opposites. We recognize that One as the only Witness to the changing phenomena of this universe. May we through that Grace go beyond darkness and delusion and realize the Truth in this very life."

Concerning the great word, *Chaitanya,* that is Consciousness Absolute. It knows itself, and knows all entities as well. One of the most illumined souls on historical record took that word for his very name, He being Lord Chaitanya, who was said to have been the perfect conjoining of Sri Krishna and Sri Radha in one form.

Chaitanya is also a name for a nondual state of *Samadhi* wherein all is known. It is often contrasted to the well known state of *Jada Samadhi* wherein the soul is so stunned by what it beholds in its deepest contemplations, that complete Self-awareness is not possible.

With these definitions in mind, an important aspect of the Jnana Matra is further revealed. But what is really demanded of the aspirant after Truth is the actual experience of this lofty station of Awareness. A seer in whom this element of the Wisdom Particle is already manifesting and expressing itself feels both intrinsically connected with all life and all things, but simultaneously detached and transcendent as well. Looking out on creation from the loftiest position possible, The Witness, whose very form is that of Chaitanya, takes up the all-pervasive nature of Divine Reality at the highest and Formless level. Perhaps Lord Buddha's powerful statement from the *Dhammapada* describes this best: *"Wide awake among sleeping souls, the wisdom-knower forges ahead of them as a powerful steed outstrips a mule. And when the wise one, having ascended to the high tower of inner perception, looks upon the world of suffering beings, he does so with an afflicted and compassionate heart. He beholds the ignorant masses as a mountaineer on the slopes espies people down in a valley."*

    Another quality that the possessor of the element of *Sakshi Chaitanya* exudes is the ability to rise above the afflictions of the world on all three levels, those called *Trividham Duhkham* or, the Three Sufferings. Whereas most beings will immediately fall into a storm of emotionalism, even at the slightest trial or sorrow, the transcendent Witness can look out upon major calamities of earth-shaking proportions without losing either mental balance or external composure. It is not callousness that enables this ability, seeing that we have just read Lord Buddha's statement above. Higher knowledge from the Intelligent Particle allows it. The chart on the facing page outlines the Three Sufferings, and the triple Peace that the Witness brings to them.

    All nine petals of the Jnana Matra, revealed on

TRIVIDHAM DUHKHAM — THE THREEFOLD SORROWS OF EXISTENCE

Chart by Babaji Bob Kindler
Property of SRV Associations

The Three Worlds (Triloka)

"Shanti" → Adhibhuta — Nature, Living Beings
"Shanti" → Adhidaiva — Celestial, Gods/Devas
"Shanti" → Adhyatma — Mental / Internal

1. Adhibautika (External Dangers)	2. Adhidaivika (Transpersonal Dangers)	3. Adhyatmika (Intrapersonal Dangers)
a) From Nature: Floods, Earthquakes, Plagues, Famine b) From Living Beings: Micro-organisms, Insects, Animals, Human Beings	a) Lower Realms: Ghosts & Spirits, Asuras, Enemies, Ancestors b) Higher Realms: Demigods, Siddhis, Devas, Devis	a) Mental: Desire, Passion, Jealousy, Fear, Greed, Depression... b) Physical Imbalances: *Datus* — Constituents (blood, flesh, bones, air, bile, phlegm) *Rasas* — Fluid essences (hormones, gastric, etc.) *Karanas* — Senses/Mind (Active & cognitive)

TRIVIDHO BANDHAH — THE THREE CAUSES OF BONDAGE | TRIVIDHO MOKSHAH — THE THREE KINDS OF LIBERATION

TRIVIDHO BANDHAH — The Three Causes of Bondage	TRIVIDHO MOKSHAH — The Three Kinds of Liberation
1. Prakrtika Bandha (Identification with the Eight Prakrtis)	1. Arising from Transcendence of Prakrti and the Pairs of Opposites
2. Vaikrtika Bandha (Bondage to the Objects of the Senses)	2. Arising from the Elimination of all Attachments
3. Dakshina Bandha (Involvement in Career, Success, & Wealth)	3. Arising from the Expansion of Knowledge

ASTADHAH SIDDHIH — THE EIGHT GREAT ACCOMPLISHMENTS

1-3. Attaining the Three Primary Siddhis (Removal of the Threefold Sorrows)

4-8. Attaining the Five Secondary Siddhis (Means to removing the Three Sorrows)

1) Contemplation of a Traditional Religion
2) In-depth Study of the Wisdom Scriptures
3) Acquisition & Comprehension of Knowledge from the Scriptures
4) Gaining Guru, Path, & Disciples/Students/Friends/Compatriots
5) Attaining Self-Purification Leading to Self-Realization

"May you fly to refuge in the Great Devi, who will cut the knot of this world asunder and free you from the threefold sorrows of existence." — Srimad Devi Bhagavatam

page 5, have now been examined in some depth. On their own, these petals represent individual powers that are responsible for everything from the projection of worlds in name and form in time and space, on down to the destruction of ignorance in the human mind. Fused together into one unit, however, they form a force of Awareness that is irresistible in its advent, irrepressible in its flow, and irreversible in its salutary effects.

This unseen wisdom unit also irradiates its translucent living rays upon all naturally intelligent beings who consciously seek the incandescent Light of Consciousness *(jyoti)*. When stilled and in their natural state, or when rendered static by the advent of Nondual *Samadhi (Nirvikalpa)* into the illumined human mind, these billions of sapient sparks settle in peacefully and blissfully, infilling the Ocean of Awareness in homogenous fashion. Contemplation of them in their abundance is the favored mead of the sage and seer enamored of Divine Reality.

Other facets of the Wisdom Particle, featured on page 5's main chart, can now be encountered. For this we will concentrate on the *Jnana Matra's* versatile movements pertinent to penetrating into the human context and bringing healing where needed, fulfillment where desired, and spiritual enlightenment where an end to all projections of the mind are aspired for and Nonduality is sought, first and foremost.

Chapter Two

The Impenetrable Cell Wall of Jnana Matra

Retentive memory, the force of sheer intelligence, projecting power, and pervading quality — these four ingredients make up the impenetrable cell wall of the Wisdom Particle. Of these four, and as far as both aspiring and impeded human beings are concerned, *Smriti,* retentive memory, is most important, because loss or lack of it is the one thing that can hide this superlative atom of conscious Awareness from view and access. The simple saying, "Don't forget to remember" applies here, and it pertains primarily to matters spiritual in nature.

In other words, remembrance is half the battle in the war against human ignorance. Of the five great impediments *(kleshas)* to Yoga (nondual union with Divine Reality), *avidya* (ignorance of one's true nature as *Atman*) is the first, and its presence causes the other four — *asmita* (egoism), *raga* (attachment), *dvesha* (aversion), and *abhinivesha* (clinging to life/fear of death) — to appear and spoil human life and endeavor. And speaking of spoilage, of the Nine "Despoilers," or *antaryayas/vikshepas* of Yoga, it is this teacher's opinion that *Bhrantidarshana* — confused vision due to weakened memory — is at the base of the other eight (stagnation, inability to make spiritual progress, immoderation, idleness, negligence, inadvertence, ambivalence, and physical disease).

These considerable obstacles in the way of real human progress are dealt with in religious life by practices such as *brahmacharya* (abstinence), *svadhyaya*, (memorization of scriptures), and *aparigraha*, (non-receiving of gifts and materials). All three of these are key to the young aspirant's maintenance of mental balance and stability, especially as individual self-effort proceeds towards further and deeper stages of spiritual attainment.

It is rather obvious how memorization of scriptures, slokas, sutras, and devotional songs will benefit the mind's memory. The practice of *svadhyaya*, alone, especially when instilled at an early age, will not only shore the youthful aspirant up for life and all its challenges, but will run deep grooves of wisdom into the mind's subtle matter that will resurface in future lives as well. This is the simple secret to why some beings have a well-developed memory early on, and others do not. To develop retentive memory in this present life, then, is what is wanted.

If it is not obvious, however, how celibacy *(brahmacharya)* and nonreceiving of gifts *(aparigraha)* help one's memory, then the answer here is also surprisingly simple. In the case of celibacy (in students and monks) and moderation (in householders), there has long been a known association in India between the retention of vital energy followed by its sublimation into the power of intelligence. Therefore, one's potential access to *Jnana Matras* and their flow will be benefitted immensely when celibacy and moderation are observed, even for any given length of time. As Sri Ramakrishna has stated in this regard, *"Honey tends to leak out of a honeycomb over time. Therefore, keep the entire comb in a jar."* One's vital energy should be retained, then, and pointed towards higher attainments rather than squandered among surface enjoyments and base sensual experiences. Stored up vital energy is tantamount to beneficial reserves useful for future contingencies.

As for the observance of non-receiving of gifts, or *aparigraha,* the point is that the mind's continual focus upon daily commerce and its material gains simply takes the emphasis off of higher leanings. By thinking of the world, its pleasures, and its objects of pleasure, the mind duly forgets all the valuable experiences it gleaned in previous lives. This pattern results in what the seers have called *"the chronic disease of worldliness."* Other than spiritual awakening due to gradual dispassion, detachment, and renunciation, there is no cure for it.

Put in even simpler terms, preoccupation with mundane matters verily buries one's previous attainments under masses of distraction, weights of worries, and shrouds of uncertainty. Amassing more than one needs or could possibly use, and dealing with all the strings attached to gifts received and reactions to gifts given, the mind gets taxed to the point of forgetfulness of both higher learning and deeper wisdom. The only dubious benefit here, if it comes in time, is the realization that happiness in this world is only a word, while all along the real loss has been that of peace of mind.

It may not be the way of the world with regard to conventional thinking to even consider the many-lifetime scenario as anything other than speculation. But this only further proves the problem of forgetfulness in the human mind. The glaring and seeming injustices around variegated human circumstances places both the vaunted laws of religious morality and the unrealistic scientific search for a utopian society on unstable and uncertain ground. On the other hand, if embodied beings knew the laws of karma, and the enlightened choices that spiritually awakened beings opt for before and at the time of their births, they would themselves begin to initiate the refinement process with regard to their present and future lives. The chart on the facing page (page 53) lays out an artistic rendering of what would be possible for such an awakened soul, and what has already come into fruition in the cases of a host of luminaries, past and present.

In the case of most beings born into the body on this earth, the canvas of their mind is a blank. Or, it is temporarily vacant until the early experiences of life begin to call from the background certain impressions and complexes that were formulated in previous existences *(samskaras)* — much like ancient paintings covered over by more recent works, then exposed again. This empty canvas of consciousness could have been painted with a colorful array of positive qualities and attributes, had the soul been aware of its own Wisdom Particles during earlier lifetimes. This would suggest mastery of consciousness, which is the singular attainment of the luminary.

The chart on the facing page (53) reveals several choices that the enlightened being avails itself of. Such a soul will gain jivanmukti in a previous lifetime, pass from the old body consciously, then take a fully conscious birth. This is accomplished by the practice of spiritual disciplines during his/her previous lifetimes.

The Palette of Conscious Future Lives

"Human being — today it is, tomorrow it is not. No one will accompany a person after death. Only actions, good and bad, follow, even after death. The result of karma is inevitable. But karma's effects can be counteracted greatly by japa and austerities." Sri Sarada Devi

- Attaining jivanmukti, Liberation, in a past Lifetime
- Selecting the country and culture of ones choice
- Assuming gender and physical body

- Spiritual practice and attainment in previous Lives
- Choosing dharmic parents prior to entering into the womb
- Arranging life-circumstances in order to neutralize karma

- Experiencing a conscious death at the end of the last Lifetime

"Ego, plus mind, plus intelligence — and adding in the five senses — make up this temporal unit called the psycho-physical being. When considering it and its powers, we must remember that when these eight facets are kept in a pure state, then Kundalini Shakti loves to sport in this amazing form." Lord Vasishtha

- Setting up the manifestation of ones work and mission in life

- Sincere compassion to help all beings gain spiritual emancipation

- Cosmic Wisdom
- Clear Mind
- Strong Intention/Resolve
- Pure Will
- Spiritual Adeptship
- Farsightedness

- Nondual perspective that transforms all appearances into Reality

"The potter puts his pots in the sun to dry, both the baked and unbaked ones. A cow happens to walk over them and breaks some of them. The baked pot shards that are broken he throws away, but the soft ones, though broken, he gathers up and shapes them into a lump. From this lump he forms new pots. In the same way, so long as a man has not realized God, he will have to come back to this earth — to the Potter's Hands." Sri Ramakrishna Paramahamsa

Chart by Babaji Bob Kindler Property of SRV Associations

Just before this dharmic soul is about to take its new body, it will look out and observe the host of couples who are desirous of having offspring. Seeing the qualities of these, it will make its choice of parents based upon other factors such as the geographical location and the best circumstances for continuing and fulfilling its life mission. For an advanced soul such as this, the benefit of all living beings is its main consideration. Other beings are born to satisfy desires, work out mixed karmas, and even wreak violence and seek revenge, etc. The *Jnana Matra* is not available to these types of souls unless they can attain the grace of an illumined being in any given lifetime.

For the luminary, the only further attainment might be the mind's expansion and activation of the state of nonduality so that deeper spiritual experiences can occur. And as the quote at the center of the chart (page 53) reveals, this unique soul will become the sporting ground for Kundalini Shakti. The best example of this in recent times is the superlative *Paramahamsa,* Sri Ramakrishna, in whom the Divine Mother fully expressed Herself.

The palette of living intelligence that the illumined soul commands is impressive, and the paintbrush of his indomitable will, amazing. The blazing colors there will be utilized to create a lifetime that is one of the abiding masterpieces of the Lord. The reader is asked look back to review the chart on page 15 and remember that the living being, *Jivatman,* is one of the Six Powers of God. It is now becoming more evident why this is so. With abilities like clear mind, strong resolve, spiritual adeptship, and farsightedness, there is no limiting the possibilities that are present and available to the living liberated soul. Plus, there is Cosmic Wisdom there, and that speaks of Wisdom Particles and their incomparable and mellifluous flows.

With the facet of *Retentive Memory* explored and studied, the next element of the cell wall of the *Jnana Matra* to focus upon is the force of Intelligence itself — or Herself, as we have just mentioned. Called **Chitshakti** in classic Yoga, and by other endearing and enduring names that fill the pages of scriptures, She is the very essence of the highest thoughts of the realized seers, and the Source of both as well.

Chit is thought, sometimes defined in English as the "stuff of the mind." The astute and observant human being has only to look at the thoughts of most beings alive today, and also notice the trend of one's own thoughts from day to day, meditation to meditation, to know that some "stuff" of the mind is not of very high quality. The "1000 Imbecilities of the Mind," as Vedanta calls them, for instance, do not sound worthy or indicative of Chitshakti at all. As Sri Ramakrishna has noted, *"The chitta, thoughts of the mind, have to be charged up by spiritual practices. If they are not they become like rain water, always seeking the lowest place to settle, but if they are, they become more like hot air balloons that rise naturally."*

Of course, the additional problem with hot air balloons are the sandbags kept inside. Casting such weights out, and at the proper time, will afford for that elevation that is so crucial for higher and more expansive views, i.e., that breathless air of heights that spiritual disciplines like study of scripture and meditation bring to the sincere spiritual aspirant. Lower views and limited perspectives, then, are to be outgrown, and this is a healthy way of proceeding. To quote Swami Vivekananda: *"Although I am in full sympathy with the various branches of religious and social work, I find specialization of work absolutely necessary. Our special branch is to preach Vedanta. Helping in other work should be subservient to that one ideal. As soon as human beings perceive the glory of the Vedanta, all abracadabras fall off of themselves. This has been my uniform experience. Whenever mankind attains a higher vision, the lower vision disappears of itself."*

The superlative intelligence associated with *Chitshakti*, then, is *"specialized,"* not ordinary; sacred, not secular; unifying, not divisive; revelatory, not obscurative. The reader is asked to look back and review the chart on page 13 regarding *Pratibha*, the flint-like intelligence of the spiritually informed mind. In addition, the chart on the facing page (57) treats *Chitshakti* in terms of *Prakasha*, revelation, and all that stands as veils to it. This chart further demonstrates the resilience of the *Jnana Matra's* cell wall.

"The eyes are located at the forehead, yet the human gaze is fixed ever downwards towards the centers of eating, drinking, and sex-life." This statement by Sri Ramakrishna refers to living beings who are under the influence of the distorting *(vikshepa)* and veiling *(avarana)* powers of *mayashakti*. Even the two eyes in the forehead, of physical design, are not seeing arightly. They are as if cross-eyed, laboring under double vision all the time. This is precisely why they see nothing clearly in the dream state as well, and are completely

Prakasha Shakti — The Revealing Power
Maya's Influence Towards Freedom

"Maya is an insentient force that, though invested with inherent powers of obscuration and distortion, nevertheless is present to drive beings towards remembrance and enlightenment. The Tantric adepts state that she covers our eyes with one hand, but leads us towards freedom with the other. This directive power is Prakasha Shakti. Prakasha is the revelatory light; Prakashaka is its revealer; Prakasya is the thing revealed."

Babaji Bob Kindler

The Three Mayashaktis

Avarana Shakti — The Power of Obscuration
* Veils the mind on individual, collective, and cosmic levels
* Is related to the guna of Tamas
* Works in conjunction with Vikshepa Shakti

Vikshepa Shakti — The Power of Distortion
* Distorts the mind on individual, collective, and cosmic levels
* Is related to the guna of Rajas
* Works in conjunction with Avarana and Prakasha Shaktis

Prakasha Shakti — The Power of Revelation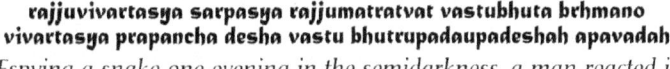
* Clarifies the mind by revealing the actual nature of things
* Is related to the guna of Sattva, and leads beyond it as well
* Exposes truth in association with Adhyaropa and Apavada

Adhyaropa - The ability of the spiritual aspirant to adroitly detect the unreal false superimposition of name and form over Brahman.

Apavada - The ability of the spiritual aspirant to, via rejection of the unreal, do away with the false superimposition of name and form over Brahman.

"Once I had entered the woods and was sitting in meditation in the pine grove when suddenly I had a vision in the form of something like a chamber door in the ground. I couldn't see inside the chamber so I tried to bore a hole in the door with a nail-knife. But as I dug, the earth kept falling into the hole and filling it. Then suddenly I made a very big opening...."

Sri Ramakrishna Paramahamsa

rajjuvivartasya sarpasya rajjumatratvat vastubhuta brhmano vivartasya prapancha desha vastu bhutrupadaupadeshah apavadah

"Espying a snake one evening in the semidarkness, a man reacted in abject fear. Upon closer inspection he saw that the illusory snake was really a rope. Similarly, a man sees the universe where only Brahman exists. The power of obscuration, avarana, causes his mind to cover Reality with the world. The power of distortion, vikshepa, makes him perceive the world as distinct from Brahman. But the penetrating power of prakasha reveals all such superimpositions and projections to be unreal."

Babaji Bob Kindler

Chart by Babaji Bob Kindler   Property of SRV Associations

blind in the deep sleep state. A fool goes into deep sleep and comes out a fool, but a seer enters deep sleep and sees the Light of *Brahman* there, and comes to know where all of nature *(prakriti)* is stored when it passes into formlessness.

So, the veiling power of *mayashakti* is thick in the unawakened soul. It is the guna of *tamas* that congeals there, as explained in the chart on the previous page. If and when there is activity in such a darksome mind, it is usually because of the rise of erratic energy, called *rajas*. This is the realm of *vikshepa shakti*, where all is other than what it seems. Caught between the veiling and the distorting powers of maya, the heavily afflicted soul knows no peace, gets no rest.

That is why the wise beings strive for *sattva guna*, the mode of balance. In that atmosphere there is a chance that the *prakasha shakti*, the revelatory power, will visit the mind. It is the presence of *prakasha shakti* that gives *maya* its trend towards freedom; otherwise, distraction and darkness are all that can be expected of life. Under the benign influence of *prakasha shakti*, however, visions are seen, scriptures are composed, divine works are carried off. Even the destruction of mass karmas on the collective level of mind can be accomplished. Suffice to say, then, and in light of our main topic under study in this book, wherever the *Jnana Matra* flows it is attended by the illumining force of revelation.

But revelation depends upon two additional factors for its gift, and these are the two other aforementioned ingredients in the cell wall of the Wisdom Particle. These are its projecting power and pervading quality.

The first, projecting power — ***Sankalpamatra*** — fashions infinite realms out of intelligence wherever it flows. That physical worlds are supposed to consist of atomic particles alone is a sleight of hand conjured by *avarana shakti*, the veiling power mentioned earlier. The real underlying consistency of objects is intelligence, and their appearance is also due to intelligence. Naive souls look at the world and see the beauty of nature; knowledgeable souls look and see atomic particles; wise souls look and see intelligence. It is with this selfsame intelligence that realized souls perceive *Brahman*, Divine Reality, in everything.

The Sanskrit word, *sankalpa*, lends new meaning to the phrase, "a loaded word." It has been described in India as being everything from a positive evil, to a boon bestowed on the god of creation by the Divine Mother. It all depends upon how it is used.

Generally speaking, *sankalpa* connotes mental projection. If the sage perceives the Cosmic Order of things in deep meditation, for instance, he is going to emerge from that state of revelation and begin to use the words "mental projection" in place of the word "creation" from that moment on. In the highest philosophical circles, it is known that you cannot create something out of nothing. Nothing does not exist. This is true for all things because of their origin in the Great Mind as intelligence. In the case of the Soul, it is nothing short of ridiculous to imagine that It is ever created; It is eternal. It does not suffer beginnings, middles, and ends — creation, preservation, and destruction. "Eternal" means transcendent of time.

The human mind, then, is engaging in *sankalpa* all the time. The Sanskrit word, *kalpanika*, means "imaginations in time," so the entire force of the mind, with all its various powers — fantasies, imaginations, conceptions, fancies, desires, day-dreaming, nocturnal dreaming, etc. — is a projection by it. Revealingly, it is only when these hazy forms of fancification turn into informed and conscious occupations like rumination, contemplation, reflection, concentration, and finally, meditation, that the deluding power in the mind begins to get shorn away, and the Wisdom Particles charge up and take on the aspect of *Prakasha Shakti*. After all, they all have the flint-like *Pratibha* within them. Their conscious flow equals concentration at its best, and the best of human endeavor, at all levels of awareness, manifests and expresses itself via that stream of Awareness.

Knowledge of the projecting power, *sankalpa*, is helpful to the aspiring soul in as much as both its veiling and revealing elements confer valuable information. To be able to recognize the mind's desire-based attraction for mental projection and thereby avoid the temptation to overly indulge in it, as well as to avail oneself of the mind's power to spontaneously shift levels of awareness at an incomprehensible speed, ensures both success in earthly endeavors and the timely fructification of spirituality so necessary for Self-realization.

Sankalpa occurs at three levels of consciousness, all correlated with the Three Worlds — gross, subtle, and causal. In the present author's previous book, *A Quintessential Yoga Vasishtha,* much is taught concerning the processes of sankalpa. Three charts appear there, the first explaining some three types of mental projection, the second describing the extent of what mental projection covers in terms of the mind's various activities, and the third being a storyboard reflecting an example of a very astute son of an illumined *Rishi* who becomes immured in the *sankalpa* process and experiences a series of lifetimes as a result.

About the three types of *sankalpa*, then, they are *mayic, lilac,* and *atmic.* The mind that is fragmented, confused, and unclear, or even merely caught in its own projections that are clear about the world but unclear about Divine Reality, is engaging all the time in *Mayic sankalpa.* The mind that has reached freedom in a previous life, and has returned to the world to sport *(lila)* in the embodied condition, as well as to be an example of how to live free, is deftly utilizing the power of *Lila sankalpa.* The great soul who uses no power at all, and who does not employ the mind for any other purpose than to exemplify nonduality and enter in and out of samadhi — that one is living in a state that might be called *Atmic sankalpa.* There is not a lot of difference between these latter two forms of mental projection. And so, a definitive measure for what one's mind is doing in accord with projections of all types is explained by Lord Vasishtha in the unique scripture, *Yoga Vasishtha.*

Concerning the three levels, or worlds, that mental projection is made of, exists on, and continues under, and generally based in desire, they are the physical world, the mind, and the intellect — or can be simply called Earth, Heaven, and Higher Heaven. In the first, on Earth *(bhurloka),* sankalpa is for the sake of food, sense objects, pleasures, and possessions. In the second, Heaven *(bhuvarloka),* the urge is for many worlds, heaven itself, and the excitement of exploring and enjoying them. In the third, called Higher Heaven (*svarloka*), it is power, glory, and pride of manipulation that is foremost.

Thus, we see that sankalpa of a rather base type pervades the minds of most living beings who assume forms among human beings, ancestors, and celestials. In addition to clarifying other levels of consciousness and other worlds within, this teaching reveals the limitations and dangers of mental projection associated with ego and its desires, higher and lower.

To complete this somewhat short exposé on the penetrating power *(sankalpa)* of the *Jnana Matra's* cell wall, it can be said that it is obvious that the aspirant must refine the mind in order to attain sankalpa of an atmic or lilac level. Utilizing the principle of *pratibha* focused on before, the chart on the facing page gives the aspirant a way of dealing with the mind in conjunction with certain challenging elements of the sankalpa process.

In accord with *pratibha*, flint-like intelligence, arise *pratibandhakas*, obstacles, and *pratibandhaka-bhavas*, their solutions. The science of *vrittis* in Yoga, which are mental vibrations like thoughts — good, bad, and mixed — are certainly all tied up with the sankalpa processes in human beings. A list of seven impeding types of vrittis are given on the chart (page 63), mental problems like dullness, anger, deception, insouciance, confusion, instability, and fragmentation.

The philosophical science of Yoga advises observation and exercise of the breathing process when there is dullness of mind. This is to be done along with *svadhyaya,* or study and memorization of scripture, for it is

❊ Some Obstacles & Solutions in Spiritual Life ❊

"Pratibhasika is the illusory reality, and Pratibha is the intelligence which is developed and honed to bring about the power (pratibandhakabhava) to destroy it, outright, along with all the impediments (pratibandhakas) in the mind which restrict the naturally enlightened state of pure, conscious Awareness."
— Babaji Bob Kindler

Pratibandhakas – Obstacles

° The Main Impeding Mental Vrittis °

1. **Vishada-vritti** – Dull vibrations which cause despondency and dejection

2. **Vitarka-vritti** – Thoughts containing demonic vibrations which foster violence

3. **Shushna-vritti** – Mental vibrations beset by falsehood and deceit, leading to suffering

4. **Vijatiya-vritti** – Turbulent and contrary vibrations which confuse and fluster the mind

5. **Kashaya-vritti** – Vibrations rising from residual impressions due to enjoyment of pleasure

6. **Manorajya-vritti** – Ungrounded vibrations which cause the mind's awareness to drift

7. **Chanchala-vritti** – Intermittent and inconsistent vibrations which cause gaps in awareness

° The Two Powers of Avarana Shakti °

1. **Asadavarana** – The power of obscuration which covers the truth of Brahman

2. **Abhanavarana** – The power of obscuration which distracts the mind from Brahman via the manifestation of lesser lights.

° The Two Processes of the Mind °

1. **Vikalpa** – The mind's unbridled tendency towards superficial fantasy and imagination

2. **Sankalpa** – The ego's improved shift towards more controlled and self-willed thinking

Pratibandhakabhavas – Solutions

Pranayama-manana – Conscious breathing accompanied by contemplation of scripture

Indriya-nigraha-nirodha – Control of the senses and restraint of negative thoughts

Yama-niyama – Practice of the moral exercises and daily observances of Raja Yoga

Darshana – Keeping holy company with the guru, sangha, and other enlightened beings

Pratyahara – Practice of withdrawing the mind from thoughts of sense objects

Dharana – Focusing inward on the immediate nature of mind and awareness

Dhyan-samadhi – Meditation, without breaks, in order to realize the continuity of Awareness

Bhavanas – Hearing, contemplating, and realizing the truth, which destroys all doubt

Aparokshanubhuti – Direct and immediate spiritual experience gained via sadhana, meditation, and samadhi

Siddhanavakyashravana – Guided study and right conclusion with regard to the scriptures

Samskara-vinasha – The destruction of subtle impressions of the mind via samadhi

Chart by Babaji Bob Kindler   Property of SRV Associations

"Using spiritual disciplines, the aspirant after perfection destroys all mental obstacles, snaps the chain of rebirth, and attains freedom from suffering."
— Sri Ramakrishna Paramahamsa

not enough to merely breathe and feel better for a few hours, then fall back into lassitude; the practitioner has to instill the temporarily pacified mind with powerful thoughts from the seers so that no such fall will occur, or if it does due to habit for a time, it falls only into a neutral state where a new impression (samskara) of study has been instigated.

It is just this type of inner work that both brings out the Jnana Matra's intrinsic wisdom power (in the case of a soul that has striven in a past lifetime) and/or continues to strengthen the cell wall of the Wisdom Particle to render it resilient again. For, the quality of the individual's consciousness is a prime factor in the ability to comprehend subtle matters (and subtle matter).

Sri Ramakrishna used to speak of "pastry-people" in this regard, referring to delicious Indian samosas and pakoras of different grades of cost and quality. In this analogy, some mind-souls, He quipped, contain cauliflower and peas and other delicacies inside. Others, have condensed milk and spices, etc., within them. But quite a few others are filled with only plain lentil paste. Unfortunately, the mind filled with only "lentil paste" does not enjoy a resilient cell wall protecting their inherent wisdom. They and their base thoughts and untoward acts can be seen and felt painfully, widely spread across the vast expanse of the Three Worlds. It was most likely pertaining to this mentally impoverished cross section of human souls that Heraclitus made his famous comment, *"Out of every 100 men, ten should not even be there...."*

Relative to this very gross level of the sankalpa process, wholly devoid of intelligence, the same psychology just outlined above can be utilized with regard to the other impediments listed on the chart on the previous page (page 63) as well. Where demonic vibrations enter into the mind, called *vitarka-vrittis*, an effort at controlling and resisting them comes to the fore. Such poison cannot be allowed to inhabit the mind, at least not for long, because impressions, like grooves in the "mind-stuff," will be left there, causing an undue return, deviation, and habitual regression to more of the same in the near future. The mind is sometimes called the "sixth sense," which should have less to do with its desire for psychic powers, and more to do with its role of master over the other and subservient "five senses." To control them is to aspire for Yoga, Union with Reality. Wisdom Particles are already and always one with this Reality. Keeping them veiled will cover up even the thought of the existence of God, as is instanced in the various cases of the worldly, the atheists, agnostics, and all the way down to demonic souls.

Shushna-vrittis are thought vibrations wrapped up in lies and deceit. They emanate, of course, from the unripe ego, not from the Wisdom Particles. The ten *yamas* and *niyamas* of Patanjali's Yoga are to be explained, learned, and observed in order that these unwanted insinuations on the mind's otherwise peaceful demeanor die away as soon as possible. Yamas such as *asteya*, noncovetousness, and niyamas like *saucha* and *santosha*, purity and contentment, will wipe away errant thoughts swiftly and easily in the sincerely seeking soul.

Other types of erratic thought vibrations can be done away with by following the methods prescribed by Yoga and other Indian Darshanas. When turbulent and contrary thoughts (*Vijatiya-vrittis*) arise in the mind, as if uncontrollably, the afflicted soul should seek out holy company with spiritual guru and sangha. Association with enlightened beings will both act as an example and prove the existence and efficacy of spirituality as the supreme path and way.

Where the attachments to insipid pleasures (*Kashaya-vrittis*) are in the way, spoiling the progress to be made in more important undertakings, the effective but difficult limb called *Pratyahara* must be mastered. This entails training the mind to detach from sense objects, both outer and inner. Soon, as the mind gets closer to its Eternal Abode, objects and their desires will fall away and seem paltry in comparison to the enlightened bounty that the Wisdom Particle, flowing easily again, reveals and confers. In other words, one should never let objects, desires, and attachments obscure or get in the way of the *Jnana Matra's* sweet and benign expression.

Ungrounded vibrations, called *Manorajya-vrittis*, are problematic for both the worldly and the spiritual. The worldly have things to accomplish too, and they cannot do so and proceed on with their evolution if the mind drifts and falls in and out of concentration constantly. For the aspirant after higher knowledge, who is through with the things of the world, breaks in study, concentration, and meditation — what to speak of the peace and bliss that come from them — are aggravating, causing the mind to slip out of sattvic balance, thus spoiling the bid for unbroken Yoga. Analyzing one's own consciousness is the method for overcoming this problem. Even the concentration one uses to perform such examination is healthy, and may lead one back to focus again. This is where the Advaitic method of *Atman Vichara*, or asking the question, "Who Am I," enters in and is beneficial.

Finally on our list (page 63), there are *chanchala-vrittis*. These are more specific to meditation, wherein the meditator suddenly loses contact with the Ishtam or the nondual Ideal/Principle, and is "gone" for any given period of time. Only after the return to normal consciousness does the aspirant notice that focus and constancy were lost, with no way to explain it. Some even draw the silly conclusion that they went into Samadhi! But it is the ability to remain in unbroken meditation that is the solution for broken meditation; one has to practice. At least the observance of the *chanchala* state will inform the practitioner of its presence, so that it can be done away with and a more homogenous Awareness can be attained. In and through it all, the Wisdom Particle, *Jnana Matra*, is waiting to be employed for the highest purpose.

To conclude this chapter, the only aspect of the impenetrable cell wall of *Jnana Matra* left to explore is its pervasive power, **Vyapakatma.** Before we close on the previous subject, however, this final word can be given. In the case of *Sankalpamatra*, the Wisdom Particle's projecting power, a distinction can be noted, and was inferred, between the ignorant being's inability to resist and refrain from unwise projections, and the illumined being's utilization of projection as penetrating power. Thus, projection out of ignorance, and projection/penetration for purposes of comprehension and unity, are two very different powers, and form an important distinction.

Pervading power, *Vyapakatma*, too, can be classed similarly. That is, and as Sri Ramakrishna used to say, "*Ignorance* (avidya) *is much more powerful than knowledge* (vidya)." This means that the penetrating force of ignorance is considerable, and it prevails in the minds of most embodied beings. And whereas their willingness to succumb to the influence of ignorance and all the suffering it brings is unfigurable, it is still a fact that most beings prefer to remain in their self-imposed bondage rather than seek freedom and the bliss that it entails. As the *Mundakopanisad* states, "*Engrossed in the ways of the ignorant, these beings childishly think that they have gained the final aims of life. But being subject to passions and attachments, they never attain to real knowledge, and therefore they sink down, wretched, when the fruits of their various deeds are exhausted.*"

However, if the soul — a rare and dignified soul — decides to search for Truth and thereby snap the chains of his/her bondage, a prolonged and challenging exposure to the permeating power of *Vyapakatma* will have to be undergone. And along this steep and difficult trajectory it will help to know that Reality Itself, called *Brahman*, is replete with this singular quality of pervasiveness. As the *Svetasvataropanisad* states, "*The Divinity who pervades everything, always dwells in the hearts of all creatures, but they finitize That nondual Presence via emotions, intellect, will, and imagination.*"

The pervasive quality of the *Jnana Matra's* cell wall is unique in that it bespeaks of perfection, of stillness, of imperviousness. The other three ingredients of the Wisdom Particle's outer membrane — protective power, projecting power, and chitshakti — are all dynamic. This suggests that in order to comprehend the incomprehensible, the aspirant on the path towards attaining the highest perfection will have to assume a deep and static immovability that simulates the nature of Brahman Itself.

For, this is the subtlemost secret of the *Jnana Matra:* its pervading power is already everywhere, and in everything. This salient fact underlies every question as the ultimate solution. Nonmovement, or what the Advaitists call *Aparinama* (nontransformation), is the backdrop of formlessness. It is the validation for meditation. It is the bestower of peace, the stabilizer for equilibrium, the reason for contentment, and the underlying meaning for all of life. Stillness is far more satisfying than activity, but only the mind that seeks peace will come to know this. Then, not only will the soul discover the *"Peace that passeth all understanding,"* but also the Bliss *(Ananda)* that informs true Love.

Chapter Three

The Essential Triputi and "The Fourth"

Referring back to our main chart on page 5, we can take up the remainder of the teachings there and find out what else the compact, powerful, yet exceedingly infinitesimal Wisdom Particle contains.

Superimposed over the Lotus we have been studying, petal by petal, lies the famous Sanskrit symbol of *Aum*, also called "The Word." By now the *Jnana Matra's* connection with The Word ought to be clear and evident, The Word being the source of origin of all projected things.

But what many beings do not know about The Word (also called the Pranava) is that each of its own three portions — "A," "U," and "M," — are *matras* themselves, and stand for a number of significant wisdom qualities that are titled *triputis* is Sanskrit. Triple attributes such as The Three Worlds, The Trinity, The Three Gateways, The Three States of Mental Evolution, The Three Gunas, The Three Types of Karma, The Three Purities, the Three Transformations, Three Types of Sacrifice, The Three Cosmic Functions, and a host of other triple aspects find their home in AUM. Further, there are the Three Phases of Time, The Three Levels of Mind, The Three Phases of the Breath, The Three Bodies, The Three Modes of Philosophy, and many more. What to speak of relatively benign principles like these, there are also difficult triputis such as The Three Stupefactions, The Three Bondages, The Threefold Miseries, The Three Obstacles to Self-Realization, and others. Coming to know these Sets of Threes provides the aspiring soul with an education like no other in the "Three Worlds."

It is possible, however, that there is no triputi more important to know than the Three States of Human Awareness, namely, waking, dreaming, and deep sleep. These are called *Jagrat, Svapna,* and *Sushupti* in the Vedic tradition. Simply put, they are a way of discovery for the aspiring human soul that soothes restless and fragmented human consciousness and effectively sidesteps the many problems rising in secularism, fundamentalism, dualism — basically whatever conventional religion, philosophy, and theology proposes and advises over vast sweeps of time.

For most embodied beings, their waking state represents all of life. Their dreams are considered figments of their imagination, and their deep sleep state is hardly even considered, much less studied — much less meditated upon. The reason for this poor assessment of the other two states of their own consciousness lies in the absence of illumination of mind and ignorance of their true nature, Atman. If their minds were enlightened as to their eternal and essential nature, the subtle realms of dreaming and deep sleep would offer up secrets without number — one of the main ones being, (and still speaking in terms of threes) that birth, life, and death are all only assumed movements of one stationary Consciousness.

Other prime revelations, such as the knowledge of the appearance of matter and form and their return into an unmanifested state in cycles — all without any real change taking place in Reality — would follow. Soon, the human mind would come to know that universal expression resides in and burgeons forth from its own consciousness (by the power of *sankalpa*, see pages 59-62), and that it does so on three levels (cosmic, collective, and individual) via the gateways of waking, dreaming and deep sleep.

In order to arrive at a fuller understanding of the Three Matras of AUM, and their connection to the Three States of Human Awareness, the chart on the facing page (page 73) can be taken up and studied. The *Mandukyopanisad* is rather the authority on The Word in the Vedic tradition, and Gaudapada, the perfected master of Nonduality, is the prime expert. Both scripture and preceptor, then, want the aspirant to begin to master their own states of awareness so that divine life can manifest on earth in the embodied condition. Unnecessary suffering finds its end there, and necessary suffering will be easier dealt with from there.

This Upanisad, only twelve slokas long, puts the teaching in terms of mastering waking (which is the "A" of Aum), dreaming (which is the "U" of Aum), and deep sleep (the "M" of Aum). Becoming keenly aware of Awareness is akin to such mastery. The problem for most beings is, as aforementioned, that the waking state is everything to them, and unfortunately, the waking state of most beings is shallow, erratic, and given to mundane preoccupations rather than to God-realization. In other words, to sit and examine internal consciousness never occurs to them. And so, as the chart opposite reveals, and Gaudapada states, they end up *"mistaking matter for Reality."*

The Three Matras of AUM in the Mandukyopanisad

"There is one Paramatman, who is all-pervading, which associates with Its projections in different ways and in different states. What is considered enjoyable in these three abodes, and the enjoyer present in these abodes, they who know these two as distinct from each other, though they enjoy, are never contaminated thereby."   — Gaudapada

The Three Avasthas – Realms of Existence

Jagrat, Waking	Svapna, Dreaming	Sushupti, Deep Sleep
"Waking is for those who mistake matter for Reality."	"Dreaming is for those who perceive Reality otherwise."	"Sleep is for those who do not know Reality at all."
A Quality of pervading	**U** Quality of being	**M** Quality of merging

1. Vishva
Cognizer of the External

"Residing in the right eye, it experiences the gross world by means of the mind and sense organs in the waking state."

3. Prajna
Cognition Amassed

"Residing in the heart, it experiences the bliss of prajna in deep sleep."

"The nonperception of duality is common to both prajna and Turiya. Prajna, though, is bound in deep sleep, which does not exist in Turiya."

2. Taijasa
Cognizer of the Internal

"Residing in the mind, it enjoys subtle realms in the dream state."

Turiya
Pure Awareness

"The syllable A leads to Vishva; U leads to Taijasa; M leads to Prajna. There is no course for that which has no syllabic portions. When the adorable seer knows the three abiding qualities in these three abodes, that great sage enters Turiya and becomes worthy of worship."

Gaudapada's Process of Meditation on the Pranava, Om

- Know that to comprehend the Pranava, Om, is to attain Brahman.
- Envision the Pranava as the beginning, middle, and end of everything.
- Contemplate Om, quarter by quarter, and then meditate upon nothing else.
- Fix the mind unwaveringly on the blessed syllable, Om, and then destroy all fear.
- Come to know the Pranava as the Lord set in the heart of all, then grieve no more.
- Know Om, the Pranava, as the lower Brahman, and the Atman as the higher Brahman.
- Perceive the Pranava as being devoid of both inside and outside, as unique and immutable.
- To know Om as portionless, yet possessed of infinite portions, is what is known as realization.

And mental delusion does not end here. The dream state, for many, only provides an escape from the challenges of life, challenges that when faced and mastered (i.e., mastering the waking state), breed both strength and noble character in the human soul. Without this strength, and the courage that accompanies it, how can the third level of awareness, namely deep sleep, come under control, what to speak even of basic recognition? For other clues on how to both perceive and correctly ruminate on one's three levels of consciousness, the reader is invited to further study the chart on page 73.

For a more direct look at the connections taught in this crucial triputi, another chart can be reviewed opposite, on page 75. The teachings here are a road map of regions that are both unknown and unexplored to most beings. To know what happens to the individual, what states he/she enters, what mechanism is taken up or abandoned from level to level, what the condition of each level is, what the results are that he/she acquires in each, and what the respective views are within these states of consciousness — all of this represents the dynamics of the inner search along this particular path.

Further, a description of Turiya, the stateless state beyond waking, dreaming, and deep sleep, is also precious. The reader can see that there are seven attributes to the fourth level, which is actually not a state or level at all, but the presence of pure Being. By the quotes of Gaudapada and others placed under each heading, the reader can surmise that Turiya is not at all an empty or boring condition of formlessness. *"Its beauty is everywhere"* is more the truth of the matter.

The Four States of Consciousness & Seven Attributes of Turiya

Chart by Babaji Bob Kindler
Property of SRV Associations

"There exists only Paramatman, the Supreme Sentient Soul, who though one and all-pervading, is aptly situated in three states of Its own devising. Ever the transcendental Witness, It enjoys (vishva) in the gross waking state through the body and senses, experiences (taijasa) in the subtle dream realms via the projecting mind, and is knower of all (prajna) in the deep sleep state via the intelligence of the heart. The Enjoyer and the Enjoyed — that one who retains awareness of nonduality, yet who knows these two to be separate, although he enjoys, is never contaminated thereby."   Gaudapada Karika

1: Jagrat (Waking State)	2: Svapna (Dream State)	3: Sushupti (Deep Sleep State)
Individual: Vishva	Individual: Taijasa	Individual: Prajna
State: Enjoyer	State: Dreamer	State: Knower
Locale: Physical Universe	Locale: Mental Realm	Locale: Causal Realm
Mechanism: Body/Senses	Mechanism: Subtle Mind	Mechanism: Intelligence
Condition: Cause / Effect	Condition: Cause / Effect	Condition: Subtle Cause
Result: Pleasure / Pain	Result: Deception	Result: Unconscious Bliss
View: False perception of Reality	View: Skewed perception of Reality	View: Noncomprehension of Reality

4: Turiya ⟶ The Seven Attributes of Turiya
("The Fourth")

Individual: Non-existent
State: All-pervasive Oneness
Locale: Brahman
Mechanism: Consciousness
Condition: Nonduality
Result: Unalloyed Bliss
View: All-Comprehending

1) Priyatvam — Indescribable Beauty
"Atman, in its dynamic phase, diversifies entities. Those who recognize Atman's imaginings perceive It's beauty everywhere."   Gaudapada Karika

2) Anantatvam — Boundless Infinity
"Perceiving the suffering of the finite world, one should turn to the Unborn, who is Infinite." Karika

3) Satyam — Unimpeachable Truth
"Atman has neither destruction nor origination, bondage nor samsara, aspiration, salvation, nor emancipation. This is the highest Truth!"   Karika

4) Shivam — Liberating Auspiciousness
"Nonduality alone is auspicious."   Karika

5) Jnanam — Illuminating Wisdom
"Atman is like intense concentration without end, but free of conceptualization." Karika

6) Shantam — Transcendent Peace
"When mind enters nonduality, its variances are seen as unreal, and Peace descends."   Karika

7) Advaitanam — Indivisible Unity
"No difference between Jiva and Atman exists whatsoever."   Karika

And that is because *"....there is no essential difference between the jiva (embodied soul) and the Atman (supreme Soul) whatsoever."* All differences are feigned, assumed, superimposed, projected, dreamed, etc., either consciously or unconsciously, depending on the awakened or still sleeping condition of the individual's own mind. Even this bare information should prompt the beings to awaken and begin seeking the perfection that lies within so as to *"be about my Father's business."*

Referring back to the main chart of this book on page 5, the reader will notice a set of *triputis (triple teachings/assignments)* within the three petals of the lotus lying underneath the Sanskrit symbol, AUM. They are basically The Three Worlds, The Three Phases of Time, and The Three Signs of Intelligent Life. All of these align with the A, U, and M of The Word, thus with the waking, dreaming and deep sleep states of human awareness. Following are more triple connections that the aspiring student can duly meditate on in conjunction with The Word, and therefore with his/her own consciousness:

A	U	M
Brahma	Vishnu	Siva
Imminent	Transcendent	Absolute
Waking	Dreaming	Deep Sleep
Speech	Life-Force	Mind
Mother	Father	Guru
Feminine	Masculine	Neuter
Activity	Balance	Inertia
Past	Present	Future
Gross Form	Subtle Form	Causal Form

It is by way of these kinds of associations and their connections, ranging from the physical universe back inside to levels of vibrating consciousness correlating with the realm of the ancestors, celestials, gods and goddesses, and even penetrating the highest, deepest lokas of the seers, the spiritual pathways of Mother India are present to illumine the minds of embodied souls and turn them towards their own best good. These connecting points, in threes, do not quit. Taking it up from the previous box —

Gross Form (Vaishvanara)	Subtle Form (Taijasa)	Causal Form (Prajna)
Five Elements	Fourfold Mind	Formlessness
Physical Body	Five Tanmatras	Nonvibration
Active Organs	Cog. Organs & Five Pranas	Equilibrium

Even the physical world and the body are given their due, and are shown to be one with Brahman, each in their own way. That man has a name for himself, and for each of his bodies in each of his three states of awareness, is not only a unique way of explaining the special nature of a human being among all other types of beings, but also suggests a way out of bondage — particularly of the mental variety.

Suffering is mainly due to limitation. If we could blast open the borders of our minds and release the unlimited spiritual potential within us, our miseries would have no more ground upon which to fester and grow. The *vaishvanara, taijasa,* and *prajna* states of our awareness, which are names for us in our external and internal realms, are described in terms of mastery rather than of bondage. They are seen as states of blissfulness rather then phases of pain and endless struggle. The entire affair, with all its processes, is a positive one, then. Joyously going forth and connecting the dots in inward fashion, the aspiring soul will break all bonds and come out of the illusion of Maya unscathed.

One of the more contemporary connections in this area of the all-important triputi was revealed by Swami Vivekananda in the late 1800s when he came to the West to bring and distribute the life-saving teachings of the Vedanta In the territories of philosophy, The Word can be utilized to comprehend the spiritual status of a soul at various stages of awakening.

On the facing page is a chart that illustrates the Three Stages of Indian Philosophy. In relation to AUM, and mankind's three states of consciousness, the teaching relates that the soul is formless before entering the womb. It is therefore, for all intents and purposes, in the Turiya state.

When it embodies, the soul manifests the "A" of The Word and gradually lives more and more in the waking state. For most of its young life it is a dualist, dependent upon parents and raised in the idea that God and mankind are two separate entities. As the soul's body and brain grow, and so long as it is not directed towards materialism by parents and society, it remembers experiences from a past lifetime and begins to awaken to its essential nature thereby. At this point it is a qualified nondualist, coming to know its connection with Divine Reality. When spiritual practices reveal the mind as an inward territory of infinite proportions, blurring the line of demarcation between God and man, the soul becomes The Soul, Atman, an Advaitin.

The Three Stages of Indian Philosophy
Ascending Steps in Religious Understanding

"Now I will tell you my discovery. All of religion is contained in the Vedanta, that is, in the three stages of Vedantic philosophy — the dvaita, vishishtadvaita, and advaita; one comes after the other."

Advaita Vedanta of Shankara — Nondualism

Some Declarations of Advaita Vedanta
God and mankind are one inseparable entity, nondifferent
All beings, all things, are nonoriginated, free of birth and death
Man's nature is divine; impure mind superimposes ignorance

"The followers of Advaita constantly discriminate, saying, 'Brahman alone is real, the world is illusory.' Their aim is to attain Nirvana. This is Self-knowledge, discussed in the Ashtavakra Samhita. It is an experience beyond the reach of ordinary men. The followers of this school, the nondualists, say, 'Soham,' I am the Supreme Self. This real Self is unattached, impervious to all dualities, whereas the ego self suffers them. If one burns wood, some ash results, but if one burns camphor, nothing remains. All the six darshanas are contained in the Advaita." Sri Ramakrishna

Vishishtadvaita of Ramanuja — Qualified Nondualism

The Three Relations between God and the Cosmos
1. Adhara and Adheya — The Supporter and the supported
2. Niyamaka and Niyamya — The Controller and the controlled
3. Sheshin and Shesha — The Lord and His servant

"According to Ramanuja, God is qualified by the universe and its living beings. These three — Brahman, the world, and individual souls — together constitute one. It is like the case of the bel-fruit whose flesh, shell, and seeds make up the fruit itself. At first one may think that the real thing in the fruit is the flesh alone. But to get the full weight of the fruit one must weigh in the shell and seeds as well. Likewise, in spiritual discrimination, one must at first separate the unreal from the real to find out the essence. Then alone will one be able to see this essence everywhere, like in the world and its living beings. Thus, one soon realizes, as with the bel-fruit, that the Reality from which we derive the notion of Brahman is the very Reality that evolves the idea of living beings and the universe." Sri Ramakrishna

Dvaita of Madhvacharya — Dualism

The Five Differences or Distinctions of Dvaita
1. God is distinct from individual souls   2. God is distinct from nonliving matter
3. An individual soul is distinct from every other   4. Souls are distinct from matter
5. Parts of matter are distinct from one another

"The proposition upon which Madhva bases his realism is that both the knower and the object of knowledge must be real, for otherwise knowledge would not be possible. The object of knowledge, then, has a reality of its own. The world is real because it is perceived as such. The fact that an object is fleeting and subject to change does not mean it is 'unreal.' As for souls, all are distinct from one another, and are distinct from God as well, though they have dependent existence in Him. To Madhva, all souls born into the world are in a state of bondage, but by continued struggle through many lives release from this bondage may be gained." Swami Prabhavananda

Chart by Babaji Bob Kindler   Property of SRV Associations

These Three Stages of Philosophy match well with specific, ongoing stages of religious growth, and are also generally aligned with the waking, dreaming, and deep sleep states respectively.

In another chart, on the facing page, this growth is put in terms of the soul lifting itself out of the root ignorance that is peculiar to living in the waking state alone, called *Jagrat*. Gaudapada calls this *"awakening from the waking state"* — an intriguing idea! Ramana Maharshi quipped that the dreaming state is dream number one, and the waking state is dream number two. These two great souls were certainly on to something.

In this chart, the reader can clearly trace the soul's growth by the grace of Lord Vasishtha, who gave us this great teaching on the Fourteen Stages of Upper and Lower Knowledge. During the first four stages of lower knowledge, all of them attended with the word "jagrat," referring to the waking state, the transmigrating soul is completely blind to its inherent divinity. It is living in ignorance and error for the most part, and accruing karma all the while.

Then, at the fifth and sixth stages, designated as "svapna" and "svapna-jagrat," basically dreaming, it begins to lift off of its limited level of thinking and living and cognizes, maybe unknowingly as yet, that all of life is dreamlike. Here, it also receives experiences from a past lifetime, or lifetimes. Importantly, the human soul begins to *"render the waking state lucid,"* as Gaudapada advises also, which is mastering the "A" of AUM.

With the advancing knowledge of the existence of pain in all embodied states, including the dream state

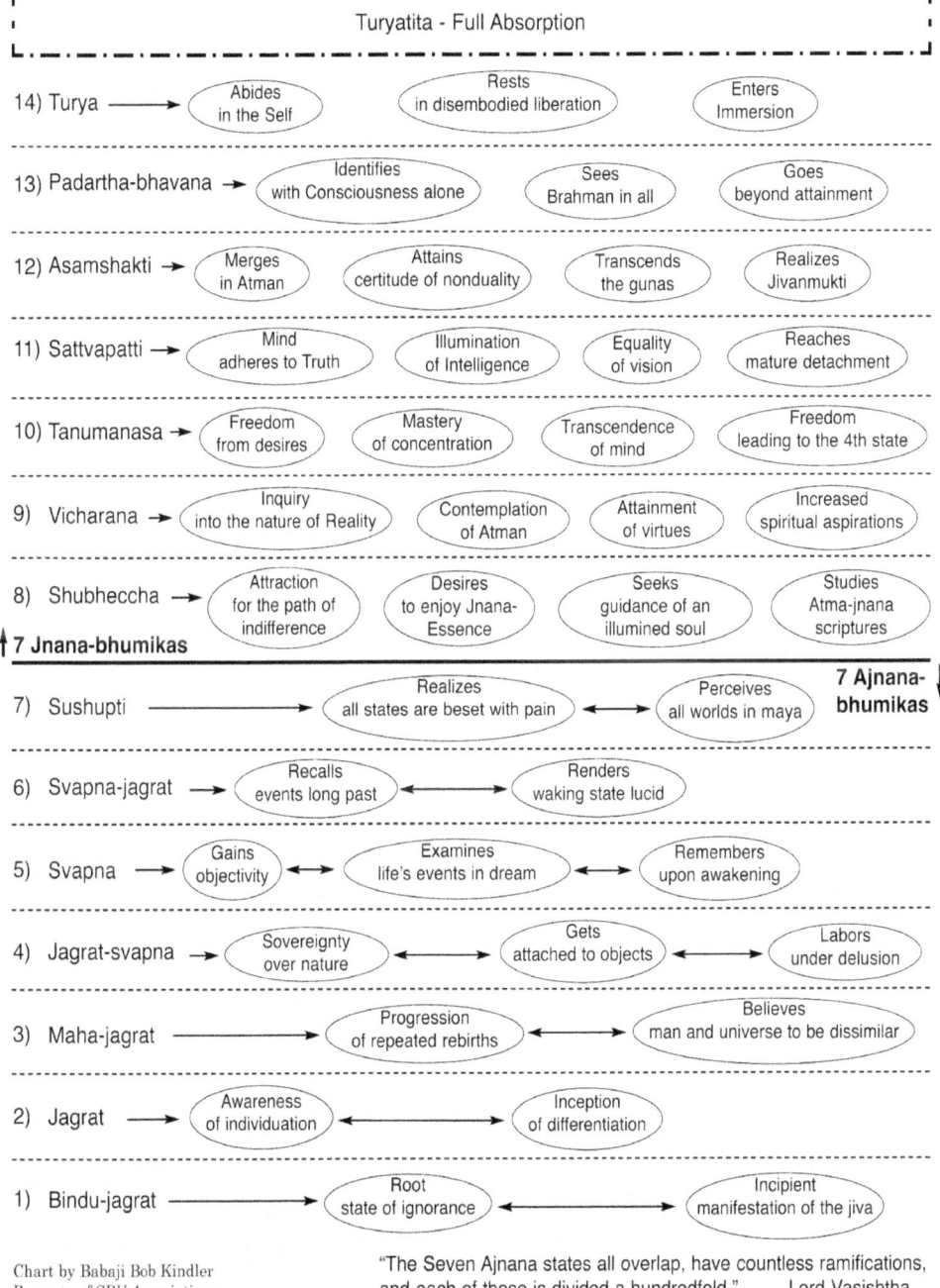

and its unattainable flights of fancy, the soul pierces through ajnana, root ignorance (by mastering the "U" of Aum), and rises into and beyond "sushupti," the deep sleep state. In other words, it becomes aware of formlessness and the bliss lying there. The *jnana bhumikas*, lands of inner wisdom, await, and when they are penetrated, an inner life opens up and dawns upon the now peaceful mind of the aspirant after Truth. The reader is invited to study the higher stages of wisdom on the chart on the preceding page (pg. 81) in order to become familiar with the path and qualities of which illumined souls avail themselves.

To conclude this chapter on triputis and Turiya, helpful mention may be made of the unusual or nonconventional way in which spiritual life proceeds as compared to all other modes of living. As mentioned earlier in this chapter, most beings would never think of examining their own consciousness, would not consider that the thoughts of their minds have any source. They would not venture to question that the waking state is all of life, and would not begin to contemplate the dream state as anything other than a figment of their own imagination. Deep sleep would not suggest a state of actual existence to them, and they probably would never identify it as the healthiest part of their day and night, being that it confers the greatest refreshment of body, mind, and spirit upon them.

These facts point to the extreme subtlety of the awakening process involved in spiritual life. Only those beings who respond to the inner call of their Soul will understand the Soul, and they are usually complete enigmas to the rest of humanity. As for the latter, they have not much recourse other than to follow the path of the world that is cut by the form-producing and destroying forces of nature, and that ends in the illusion of death amidst the dense objects of insentient matter. As Swami Vivekananda has written – and it is worth repeating:

"In the world, all things are done by people guided like lifeless machines. There is no mental activity, no unfoldment of the heart, no vibration of life, no flux of hope; there is no strong stimulation of the will, no experience of keen pleasure, nor the contact of intense sorrow; there is no stir of inventive genius, no desire for novelty, no appreciation of new things. Clouds never pass from this mind, the radiant picture of the morning sun never charms this heart. It never even occurs to the mind if there is any better state than this; where it does, it cannot convince; in the event of conviction, effort is lacking; and even where there is effort, lack of enthusiasm kills it out."

Chapter Four

Stream of Consciousness and Turiyatita

Throughout the pages of this small book, some of the many aspects of the Wisdom Particle have been presented and explained (see repeat of the main chart on the facing page). Now we are to consider the profound question, that with so much power and content present in a single atom of wisdom, how much force will be present in a stream of such particles, and what will be the effect of bringing together such a combined force and concentrating it. And to what end should this concentrated power be turned? The seer will use it towards opening the heretofore closed doors leading to the direct vision of God. This Wisdom Way is called "Stream of Consciousness" in some Eastern traditions.

Put in a way that any scientific mind might find intriguing, a single physical atom contains a force that is unimaginable to the mind, until that force is released by splitting it. Also unimaginable, though of a much more subtle nature, is the inward force that is generated by the splitting of the Wisdom Particle. Basically, darkness is shattered, ushering in the Light of Intelligence which is the penultimate source of all Existence.

In Yoga, this unique focus of mind, called Stream of Consciousness, is indicated as *Samyama*. It is the combination of the sixth, seventh, and eighth limbs of Yoga, namely concentration, meditation, and samadhi. The adept yogi utilizes such a rare amalgam to uncover the secrets of anything he wants to know, usually, of

ॐ Jnana Matra — Atom of Wisdom ॐ

"The bodies of beings which appear in the form of a framework of bones and sinews, is the self of the nature of food. Further within, is the self of Prana, split into five. Deeper still is the self of the nature of mind, different than these. Even deeper than it is the self of the nature of intelligence. At the deepest of all distinct levels is the self of the nature of Bliss....."

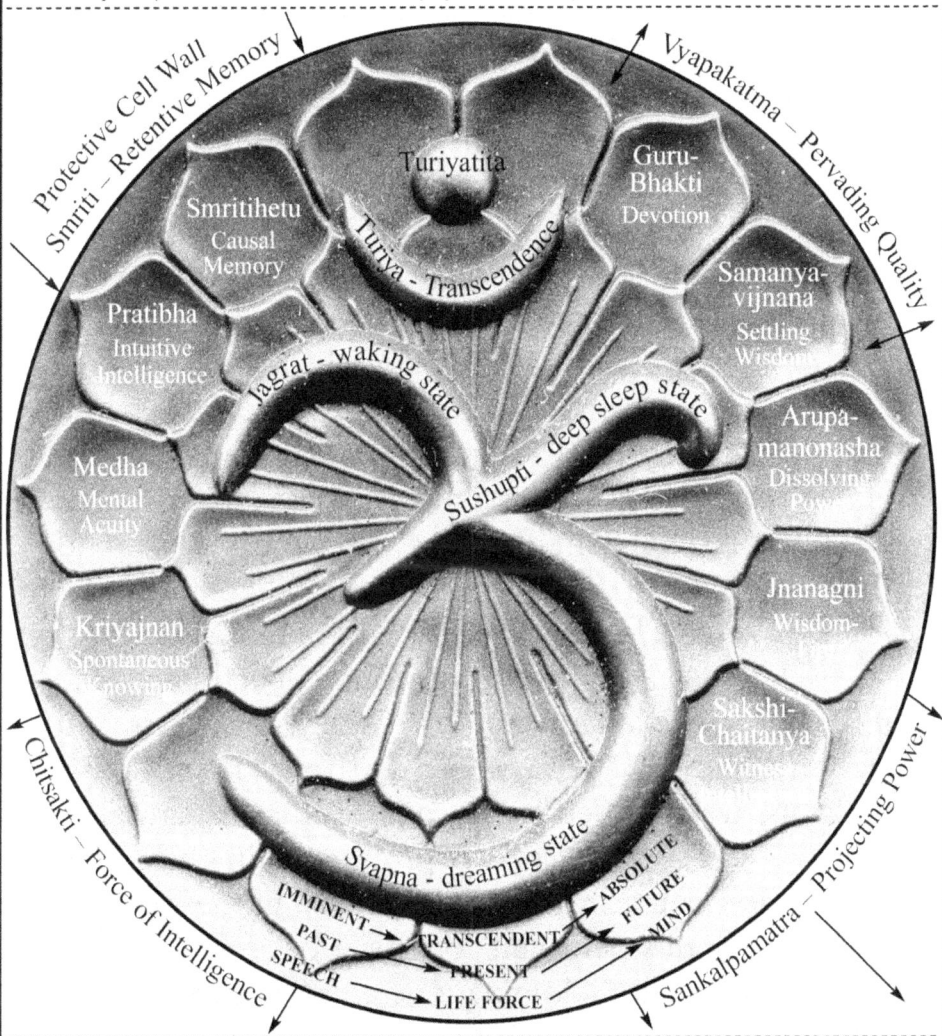

"....food is pervaded by vital energy; vital energy is pervaded by mind; mind is pervaded by intelligence, and that ever happy intelligence is pervaded by Bliss. This self of Bliss is pervaded by Brahman, the Witness, the innermost of all. Brahman is not pervaded by anything else. Neither by action, nor by begetting children, nor by anything else, only by knowing Brahman, does one attain Brahman."
Katharudra Upanisad

ॐ   Chart by Babaji Bob Kindler   Property of SRV Associations   ॐ

course, of a subtle and inward nature, related to God-vision.

But what is that unseen inner atmosphere like, and what does it hold? Why is it so difficult to penetrate and experience? The chart on the facing page has been designed to reveal in part both the pathways that run through consciousness at its many levels, and also to show what potential blockages might be encountered in such an unusual undertaking.

The human body has many thousands of nerve passages that conduct energy to its various parts. As all of the quotes from the Upanisads on the chart state, each of these physical nerves contain a multitude of subtle nerves that go unnoticed. Particles of prana, life-force, flow along these. As these gain subtler and more refined levels of awareness, there appears from hiding the flow of Intelligent Particles that embue the mind with its power of thought, conception, genius, envisionment, etc. This is the real stream of Consciousness.

The seven lokas are pictured up the left hand side of the chart, the lower three correlating with earth and heaven. The passageways (nadis) shown there, like a roadmap, are impeded by the density that is natural to lower realms where desire is prominent in the mind. The Wisdom Particle is hard to manifest in these worlds due to the soul's penchant for trivial occupations such as pleasure, wealth, domination, and the like. These worlds also correspond with the three lower chakras, all seven shown running up the middle of the chart. Below, eating, drinking, and sex life occupy the mind.

In addition, the thick and deflecting *Vishnu Granthi*, a diaphanous membrane whose tenebrous design obscures higher Reality, functions there, reject-

Lokas, Nadis, and the Transmigration of Souls

"In the heart dwells the Atman. There are a hundred and one nerves centered there, and in each of those are a hundred more, and each of these branch into seventy-two thousand nadis. In all of these the Shakti Power flows." Prasnopanisad

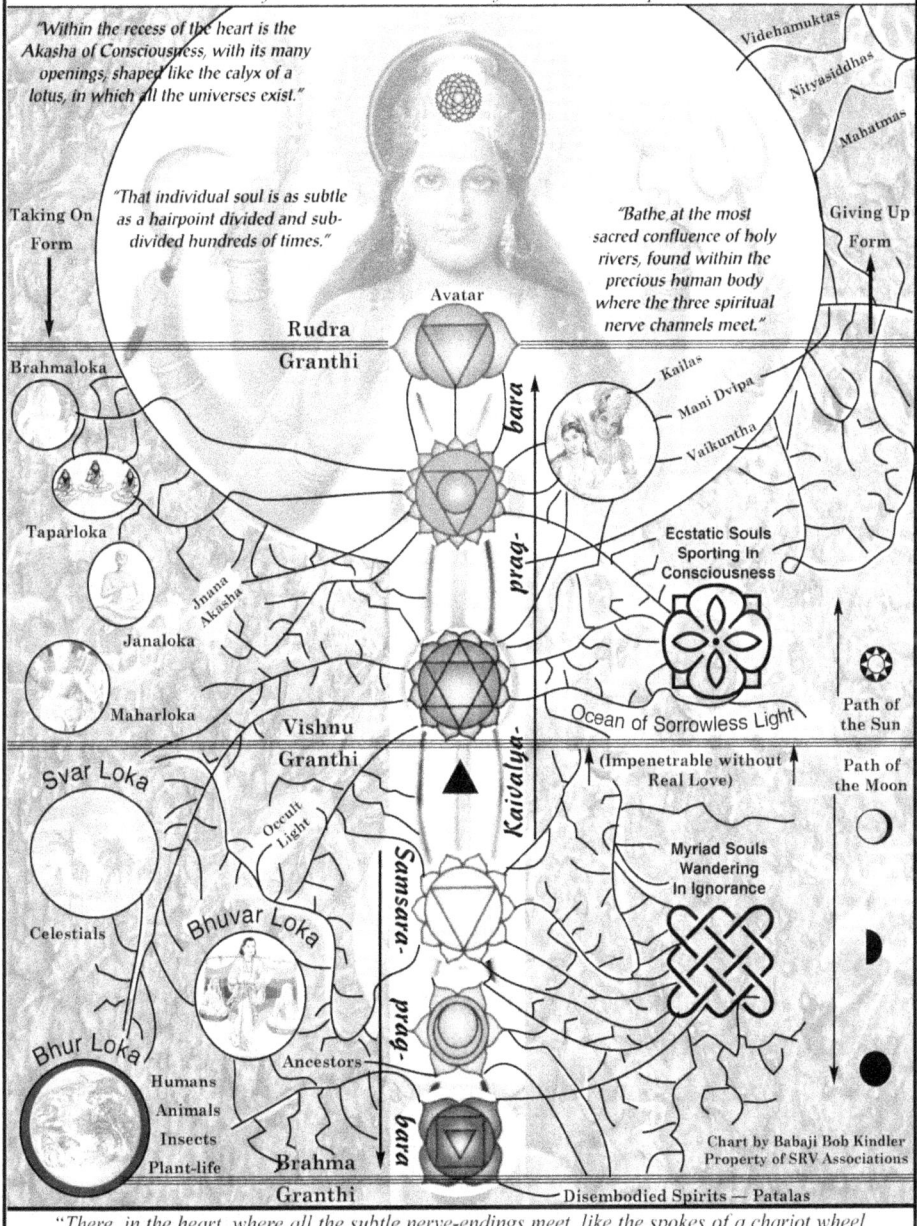

"There, in the heart, where all the subtle nerve-endings meet, like the spokes of a chariot wheel at the hub, abides the Atman, stationary, but becoming manifest. Meditate on that Self as AUM, and Godspeed to you in crossing over to the farthest shore beyond darkness." Svetasvataropanisad

ing the aspiring and rare soul's occasional bid for subtler ground. This impediment in the mind ensures that those beings who are still attached to gross preoccupations will remain in transmigratory cycles, wandering the three lower worlds in Maya where ancestors, human beings, animals, insects, and plants all make their habitation. Only the presence of mature love will allow for penetration of this barrier in consciousness, freeing the soul to attend worlds and levels that will keep it out of physical embodiment.

When the Vishnu Granthi is transcended (still referring to the chart on page 87), the soul finds itself occupying the four upper lokas, which are like dreamscapes within the collective mind. They are not locations in physical space and, in fact, do not have physical dimension at all. By way of inadequate metaphor, like huge amounts of information stored in a memory chip, similarly, all the sights, sounds, landscapes, living beings, and such, abide within these internal spaces, or *akashas*, adding no mass or volume whatsoever.

And it is much more evident here that everything is made of intelligence, especially due to the presence of subtle bliss that pervades all quarters as a unique kind of living, scintillating, Light. The rapt soul "moves" therein by a combination of psychic prana and the subtle mind's intelligence, bilocating here and there with a swiftness that is incomprehensible.

And this is where the flow of Wisdom Particles begins to present itself as a Stream of Consciousness. Those souls who are not yet through with enjoyment, albeit of a much subtler nature, will use these Intelligent Particles for the enjoyment of bliss. But others, more keen on drinking ambrosial Nectar *(amrita)* of the rarest and sweetest variety from the Source, will traverse these four higher worlds, riding on the Stream of Intelligent Particles that course, like powerful rivers, towards the Ocean of Satchitananda with its all-attracting Light *(Jyoti)* and Sound *(Nada)*.

But here is another Granthi, like a causal membrane, impeding the advanced souls's progress towards its desired end in blissful Formlessness. This is the *Rudra Granthi,* and it both signals an end to the assumption of form, and tests the soul's adamancy towards attaining such a rare state. All levels of inward awareness have guardians, or "watchers at the gate," and the guardians of this final Gate are the most illumined of souls. At the portal of the seventh chakra is where Avatars make their home, moving in and out of form with an adeptness that far surpasses the abilities of most beings.

While studying the spiritual wisdom-lore of India, answers to questions like "What happens after death" simply fall away. Doubts as to the existence of and the nature of the human soul also disappear. The Soul is eternal, and as long as it desires to play in form, so long will it do so — in numerous worlds, not just the physical one. The chart on page 87, then, though a limited representation and description of the inner worlds, will suffice to acquaint the seeker of higher wisdom with a blueprint of such lokas, or akashas, and the network of living passageways that connect them. Particularly, the vehicles upon which souls will ride, namely, Wisdom Particles in streams, will get revealed and utilized by awakened souls in meditation. Even here on Earth, some mature beings have awakened their Intelligence and found out its many and beneficial uses, especially for the service of God in mankind.

The regions beyond the *Rudra Granthi* (referring again to the chart on page 87), speak of a timeless place that can only be called *Turiyatita*, or That which is beyond even Turiya. Waking, dreaming, deep sleep, and Turiya are the four states of mankind's consciousness. But beyond The Fourth there lies what all the seers will leave unnamed, unformed, and unnumbered. All that might be said is that It is totality, It is all-encompassing. It is formless, but it can break into forms. It is nameless, but takes on many names. It transcends all levels of space, yet all of space with its innumerable boundaries — even the idea of space — lie within It.

In It are resting the fully absorbed Beings called *Videhamuktas*, supreme Souls called *Mahatmas*, and ever-perfect Ones called *Nityasiddhas*. The Divine Mother, the *Mahashakti*, reserves this infinite sweep of Light and Bliss for Her own place of formless abidance. It is the boundless sky of Her own inmost Heart. As the Upanisads say: *"In the sky of the heart, the luminous city of Brahman, the Atman is established, clothed in mind and guiding life and body. By perfect Knowledge of That the wise realize the state of blissful Immortality."*

Sanskrit Glossary

Abhinivesha — Fear of death, or clinging to Life, which is one of the five kleshas, impediments to Yoga. The Father of Vedanta calls it the fifth and lowest hell a soul can descend to.

Advaitic — Referring to Advaita, the nondualistic philosophy of the Vedanta.

Ajnana — Ignorance of one's true nature as Atman; the opposite of jnana, knowledge.

Ananda — The unalloyed, uninterrupted Bliss of Awareness.

Anandamayakosha — The sheath of bliss, or conceptual ego structure, the subtlest of the Five Sheaths of human existence as explained in the Adhara System of Vedanta.

Annam — Food; particle; matter.

Annamayakosha — The sheath of food, or the body, which is the grossest of the five coverings over Atman.

Antaryayas — Obstacles; impediments; the chitta-vikshepas, sometimes called the Nine Distractions to Spiritual Life in Yoga.

Anu — Atom; of minute size.

Anubhava — True Being; the direct perception of Divinity which is the result of self-effort and Grace; after shruti, hearing the Truth, and yukti, contemplating the Truth, it is the third of a succession of Vedantic practices which allows for the direct perception of Reality.

Aparavidya — Lower knowledge, relative knowledge, such as secular subjects, as opposed to knowledge of Reality.

Aparigraha — Defined as "nonreceiving of gifts," it is one of the ten yamas and niyamas of Patanjala Yoga which brings freedom from the double-edged problem of ownership and expectation. It is a prerequisite to the successful practice of yoga.

Aparinama — Nontransformation, describing the perfect and changeless nature of Brahman.

Aparokshanubhuti — Direct spiritual experience proceeding from one's own matured and consummated sadhana practice.

Apaurasheya — Not of human authorship, used often in reference to the scriptures of Sanatana Dharma.

Archa — Symbol; one of the four ways in which God can be perceived, i.e., through forms as symbols of Reality.

Arupa-manonasha — The powerful truth-element in the mind that dissolves all concepts and ushers in formless Awareness.

Ashtanga — Literally, "eight-limbed," quite often referring to Patanjali's eight-limbed Yoga system.

Ashtangika — Of eight parts, as in reference to Lord Buddha's Eightfold Path.

Astika — A reference to the orthodox systems of Indian philosophy, as contrasted to Nastika, the non-orthodox ones.

Atmajnan — The highest wisdom of the Eternal Self, Atman.

Atmic — Having to do with the Atman, the Supreme Soul of man.

AUM — The sacred syllable of Brahman; the primal vibration which is the sound symbol for Brahman, Ultimate Reality, and which is an essential element in all systems of Hindu Philosophy. From this primal sound come all aspects of the creation, yet being beyond the manifest universe it is the bija or sacred symbol for formless Reality Itself.

Avarana — Veiling power of Maya that obscures Reality.

Bhagavad Gita — The sacred wisdom song of Sri Krishna, which is one of the three most hallowed scriptures in Indian religious tradition.

Bhajans — The many devotional songs of India that possess deep and profound lyrics of love and wisdom.

Bhrantidarshana — Unclarity of the mind, especially in matters pertaining to the philosophical understanding that underlies Existence.

Bhumika — Step or stage; a ground or level of progress.

Bhurloka — The realm of physical objects, and the first of seven inward-reaching levels of consciousness, and the plane of physical beings — humans, animals, insects, and plants — corresponding to the Muladhara chakra.

Bijams — Seed syllables which form an essential part of a mantra, and that help invoke the presence of God through a particular mode or aspect.

Bodhi — Higher Intelligence.

Chaitanya — Pure, conscious Awareness, which is Supreme Reality in Indian religion and philosophy.

Chanchala — Erratic; restless; unsettled.

Chitta — "Stuff of the mind," meaning its thought, concepts, content, projections, imaginings, etc.

Chitshakti — The Divine Mother as the power of pure Intelligence.

Darshana — Paths of clear seeing, referring to the Six Orthodox Darshanas of India — Sankhya, Nyaya, Vaisheshika, Yoga, Purva Mimamsa, and Uttara Mimamsa (Vedanta); attending upon a holy person for spiritual instruction.

Desha — Space, often cited with kala, time, and nimitta, causality.

Devatmashakti — The divine dynamic, sentient power in everything, everywhere.

Devi — The Goddess, the "devis" if She appears in Her many aspects.

Dhammapada — The scripture of original Buddhism, consisting of teachings of the Buddha gathered by the Arhats of the tradition after his passing into Nirvana/Samadhi.

Dharma — Divine Life, lived in accordance and observation of the precepts, laws, and axioms of dharma.

Dhyanam — Meditation proper, which is the seventh of eight limbs of traditional Yoga.

Gazals — Classical religious folk songs of India.

Gunas — The three gunas of *tamas*, *rajas*, and *sattva*, which correspond to the principles of lassitude, restlessness, and balance in the human mind. All three, even balance (sattva), are to be transcended, as their presence signals disequilibrium, which ushers in the worlds of name and form in time and space.

Guruanushashana — Taking refuge with a Guru, which is one of the Three Great Sources, along with studying the revealed scriptures and gaining one's own spiritual experience.

Hatha — A school of Yoga focused on body postures and breathing exercises, whose original purpose was to strengthen the body and purify the nervous system so as to help make them fit for spiritual life and meditation. In later centuries, and especially in present times, the system's aims have degraded into the search for bodily health, occult powers, and longevity. As Svatmarama states in his *Hatha Yoga Pradipika* (16th century), *"Raja Yoga begins where Hatha Yoga leaves off."*

Ishtam — The Chosen Ideal upon whom the devotee meditates in the shrine of the heart, realizing an ineffable Presence in deepest contemplation.

Ishvara — Same as Ishtam, and referring to the Divine Personality of God with form; one of the five seats of the Devi.

Ishvariya — The declaration that revealed scriptures originate and proceed from Ishvara.

Iti Iti — Literally, "All this, All this," referring to the realization that "All is Brahman," attained after practicing the discipline of Neti Neti, "Not this, Not This."

Jada — Literally, stationary, or inert. Also, stunned, as in the type of samadhi that leaves the meditator in awe of all that is seen within during revelation and realization.

Jagad Mithya — The declaration that the world is false, or is unreal without the presence of the reality of Brahman (Brahman Satya)

Jagrat — The first of four states of a human being's awareness, that of waking consciousness.

Jivatman — The Atman existing in the form of the embodied soul, but as yet unrealized.

Jnanagni — The Fire of Wisdom that awakens the soul spiritually.

Jnanam — Wisdom, specifically of the spiritual type.

Jnana Matras — Particles of pure Wisdom.

Jnana-shashtras — The Wisdom scriptures of India.

Jyoti — The Light of Pure, Conscious Awareness.

Kala — Time; a name for Siva.

Kali — The Divine Mother of the Universe in Her four-armed form, worshipped by Sri Ramakrishna Paramahamsa; the consort of Lord Siva from the Tantric viewpoint.

Kalpanika — The mind's imaginings in time.

Kashaya — Hidden impressions of past pleasurable experiences that linger in the mind, keeping it from samadhi and higher spiritual states.

Katharudra Upanisad — One of the 108 Upanisads which are the source scriptures of the Vedanta.

Kriya — To act; in Tantra, spontaneous divinely-oriented action; internal rising of Kundalini Shakti which produces certain external effects on the body and mind; practice aimed at higher understanding with regards to spirituality.

Kriyajnan — Spontaneous Wisdom.

Kundalini — Literally, "coiled up," referring to the spiritual potential in mankind which lies dormant in the Muladhara Chakra.

Lila/Lilac — Sportive play of consciousness in form.

Loka — A realm of existence, which, unlike the physical planets in outer space, exist within, and which are gradated into various levels, hosting ancestral, celestial, subtle, and causal beings.

Lokas — A collection of internal realms.

Mahat — Referring to the Great Mind, or God's Mind, which in the Sankhya Yoga system, is the causal hub of all that is formless, and which later gets projected into form.

Mahatattvas — Literally, "Great Principles," such as a supreme station like The Word, AUM.

Mahavakyas — The four main nondual declarations of the Upanisads, namely: Tat Tvam Asi; Ayamatma Brahma; Prajnanam Brahma; and Aham Brahmasmi.

Manana — Contemplating the teachings of the scriptures and guru in the mind — manas.

Mandukyopanisad — A major Upanisad made all the more important by Gaudapada's Karika or commentary on it. Its teachings explain the four quarters of the sacred bija Aum, and transmit the essence of nonduality called Advaita Vedanta.

Manomayakosha — The sheath of mind, being one of the five sheaths of the Adhara system in Vedanta.

Manorajya — Referring to the constructing of mental kingdoms via sankalpa, often called cloud-castles in the sky of mind.

Mantras — A collection of Sanskrit word formulas which aid the

Vedic priest in performing worship, and which help the spiritual aspirant purify, refine, and clarify the mind, preparing it for samadhi.

Matras — Quintessential particles, especially those consisting of meaning and intelligence found in sacred words and scripture.

Mayashakti — The Divine Mother as the power of illusion and obscuration, and as the One who removes these from human consciousness at the auspicious time.

Mayic — Of, about, or referring to anything that is of the realm of name and form in time and space, based in causation — Maya.

Medha — Intellect and its power of retentive memory; the goddess of intelligence.

Medhakendra — The loving heart informed by the knowing intellect.

Moksha — A state of freedom always at hand; for the soul caught in the illusion of finitude, it is liberation from all bondage.

Mukhyaprana — The essential constituent in the five forms of prana, which, when flowing, conduces to perfect health in the body. This health, obtained from taking sanctified food with a reverential attitude, is a sign that the mukhyaprana is ready to be refined via spiritual disciplines and transformed into Ojas.

Mukti — Liberation, or the state of freedom always at hand.

Mulavidya — Root ignorance, primal ignorance.

Mundakopanisad — Literally, the "cutting edge of a razor," this Upanisad gives teachings designed to cut away ignorance from the mind. Its profound authority comes from the fact that its wisdom, a direct transmission from the god Brahma, is given by the great rishi Angiras to the famed disciple Saunaka.

Nadis — The overall network of thousands of subtle nerves running through the human body/mind mechanism.

Nama — Name, as an aspect of maya, or covering power, usually conjoined with form, rupa.

Naren — Short for Narendranath, which was Swami Vivekananda's given first name.

Neti Neti — "Not this, Not this," referring to the practice that the aspirant does in order to rid the mind of all that is not Real.

Nididhyasana — After shravana, hearing the Truth, and manana, reasoning about It, it is the third and highest level of comprehension in Vedanta sadhana which involves realizing Truth. Its attainment signals enlightenment while lack of its attainment shows the need for deeper insight. Those who have merely heard the Truth are novices and beginners. Those who reason about Truth are sincere aspirants and, at a higher stage, jnanis or wisdom knowers. Those who have experienced what Truth epitomizes are the true luminaries and are rare.

Nirvana — State of total absorption into Reality, like Nirvikalpa.

Nirvichara Samadhi — Samadhi free of mental vibrations and thought-forms.

Nirvikalpa — Literally, "beyond all thought forms" including time, equating to the deepest formless samadhi, nondual in essence.

Nirvitarka Samadhi — Samadhi free of intellectualization.

Niyamas — The five preliminary spiritual observances – purity, contentedness, study of scriptures, austerity, and devotion to God – practiced by the aspirant of classic Yoga prior to sitting (asana) and breathing exercises (pranayama); also, the ten niyamas of Tantra.

Ojas — The spiritual power which culminates as a result of commingling the ingestion of sanctified food with recitation of mantra, heightened vital energy, and spiritual disciplines.

Om — Same as AUM, the most sacred bijam or seed syllable, which is seen as the Word of Brahman sporting a myriad of connotations and blessings.

Omkara — Om, or AUM, as the cause of all manifestation.

Paramahamsa — "Great Swan," a name for a unique type of illumined soul who is simultaneously a superlative teacher and a past master of spirituality.

Paravidya — Higher knowledge, spiritual wisdom of revealed scripture and direct spiritual experience – as contrasted to ordinary (dualistic) scripture and intellectual knowledge (aparavidya).

Patanjali — The founder, father, or systematizer of the classic Yoga of Patanjala.

Prajnaparam — Supreme Intelligence, which was a name that Lord

Buddha used for Formless Reality.

Paurasheya — The opinion that revealed scripture originates in and proceeds from the finest human intellect.

Prakasha — Luminosity; Light in the spiritual ether.

Prakasha-shakti — The revelatory power.

Pranamayakosha — The vital sheath; life-force as a covering over Reality.

Pranava — Another designation for Om, signifying it as the origin of prana in all its forms.

Pranidhana — Self-surrender to one's Chosen Ideal.

Pratibha — Flintlike intelligence that resists maya and precedes matter.

Pratibhandika — The power of obstruction in the mind.

Pratibhandikabhava — The power of awakened intelligence that removes obstructions in the mind.

Pratibhasikasatta — Unreal or apparent dream-reality.

Prati-tantra Siddhanta — Involving looking at various doctrines as separate and contradictory.

Rajas — The guna of restlessness

Rakhal — Swami Brahmananda's given first name.

Ramachandra — The Divine Incarnation of the Treta Yuga whose heroic actions and superior teachings appear in the Adhyatma Ramayana and other scriptures.

Ramana Maharshi — The seer of Arunachala who was a contemporary exponent of Advaita Vedanta, and a supremely realized Soul.

Rishis — Illumined souls of the Vedic period in India who were seers of the Truth, and whose descendants distilled the ancient wisdom into sacred texts like the Upanisads.

Rupa — Form, an aspect of the covering power of maya, usually used in conjunction with name, nama.

Sadhana — Specialized spiritual exercises and disciplines which qualify the sincere aspirant for awakening to the presence of the chakras in the gross, subtle, and causal bodies, all leading to realization of nondual truth and samadhi.

Sahaja-tantra Siddhanta — Acknowledging the innate unity of all paths and religions.

Sahasrara — The highest center of awareness, called the crown chakra, located at the top of the head.

Sakshi — The Witness of all phenomena.

Sakshi-chaitanya — The nondual Consciousness that transcends and witnesses all beings and phenomena.

Samadhi — Any of a host of rare spiritual experiences, usually of the wisdom variety but not exclusive of devotional bhavas and moods, wherein the practitioner beholds levels of inner consciousness leading up and into the nondual state.

Samanya-Vijnana — Higher Wisdom and its settling power, which allows the mind to enter peaceful states of Awareness.

Samskaras — An important word in Sanskrit and Indian philosophy referring to impressions left in the mind by repetitive past actions which, in the case of negative impressions, and when left unneutralized, cause the transmigrating soul (mind complex) to return to rebirth again and again.

Sananda — Literally, 'with bliss'; a blissful state of awareness which is one of the four lesser states or conditions of Samprajnata Samadhi.

Sanchita — A type of karma that was formulated from actions in past lifetimes.

Sangha — A group of spiritually-minded devotees and practitioners.

Sankalpa — The vibrational activity of the mind complex which sets in motion worlds in space and time, all projected at the cosmic, collective, and individual levels in conjunction with one another.

Sankalpa Matra — A particle of intelligence that assists the luminary in projecting lives that are peaceful, harmonious, and balanced; projecting power of the Wisdom Particle.

Santosha — Contentedness. One of the ten yamas and niyamas of Patanjala Yoga which provides for balance and peace of mind.

Saradananda — In reference to Swami Saradananda, who was one of the sixteen direct disciples of Sri Ramakrishna Paramahamsa.

Sarat — Short for Saradananda, as he was affectionately called.

Sarva-tantra Siddhanta — Looking at doctrines, paths, and religions as complementary and supportive.

Sasmita Samadhi — The samadhi of yoga which is still attended by the sense of ego, therefore not yet formless or nondual.

Satchakras — The seven spiritual centers of the Kundalini Yoga system.

Satchitananda — Pure Being, pure Consciousness, pure Bliss Absolute; a name for the formless Brahman.

Satya — Truthfulness; one of the five yamas of Yoga.

Saucha — Purity. One of the ten yamas and niyamas of Patanjala Yoga which allows the aspirant to experience higher states of Consciousness.

Savichara Samadhi — A samadhi of Yoga which is attended by reasoning and deliberation.

Savitarka Samadhi — A samadhi of Yoga which is accompanied by intellectual rationalization.

Seva — Service, as in service around the ashram, service of the guru, and serving God in mankind.

Shankara — The great Advaitin whose scriptures and commentaries figure as one of the highest authorities in Vedanta philosophy.

Shishya — The disciple of a Guru.

Shravana — Hearing the Truth, which is the first of the three Proofs of Truth.

Shruti — Scripture of the most authoritative kind, superior to Smriti and Itihasa; to be heard.

Shuddhi — Purity, usually taught in three modes: of location/atmosphere; of action; of mind.

Shushna — Deception.

Siddhi — Occult power, as in the asta-bala-siddhis which seekers after Truth and Enlightenment stay away from.

Siva — The Lord of Wisdom, and third of the Hindu Trinity of primary Deities; one of the five seats of the Devi.

Slokas — Statements which make up a scripture.

Smritihetu — Causal memory, such as of one's previous births.

Stotrams — Stately musical compositions, simple in their musical content, but containing profound lyrics, usually of a nondual nature.

Surya — The God of the Sun, used as an epithet in both a physical and a cosmic sense.

Sushupti — Deep sleep state, often correlated with formlessness, and the "M" of Aum.

Sutra — A Sanskrit verse, as in the Yoga Sutras.

Svadhyaya — Study, recitation, and memorization of scripture as a prerequisite to other spiritual practices like asana and pranayam, and pratyahara. It is one of the ten yamas and niyamas of traditional Yoga (Patanjala).

Svapna — The dream state, or second of mankind's three states of consciousness (waking, dreaming, and deep sleep), associated with the "U" of Aum.

Svarloka — The realm of higher heavens, and the third of seven inward-reaching levels of consciousness which sport gods and goddesses and those beings who gather around them — corresponding to the Manipura chakra.

Svarupa — Essence, meaning pure Consciousness or Awareness.

Svetashvatara — The name of one of the more recent Upanisads, containing teachings of powerful merit and boundless scope.

Swami Brahmananda — Known as Rakhal, and also as a Jagad-Guru, world teacher, he was one of the sixteen direct disciples of Sri Ramakrishna Paramahamsa, the Avatar of this Age.

Taijasa — The second of four states of consciousness described by Vedanta, called the dream state.

Tamas — One of the three gunas, or modes of nature, signifying inertia in nature and slothfulness in the mind.

Tantras — Literally, "that which saves," they are a collection of scriptures which, along with the Upanisads, Bhagavad Gita, Brahma-sutras, and others, make up the Sanatana Dharma — the eternal religion of India.

Tejas — The light of refined Awareness; radiance.

Triputis — Triple principles that are fundamental in teaching spiritual truths.

Trividham Duhkham — The three forms of suffering as enumerated in the Lord Kapila's Sankhya Yoga system.

Turiya — Literally, "The Fourth," referring to the fourth state of Awareness beyond waking, dreaming, and deep sleep. It is synonymous with the highest Samadhi, i.e., Asamprajnata in Yoga and Nirvikalpa in Vedanta.

Upanisad — The distillation of Vedic Wisdom, specifically around nondualism or Advaita. The word has been defined as "the proximity to the spiritual luminary which loosens the knot of ignorance and ushers in freedom."

Upanisads — A collection of 108 still existing scriptures of Mother India, considered as primary scriptures which must be heard.

Uttara Mimamsa — The Vedanta system, or darshana.

Vaishvanara — The first of four states of consciousness described by Vedanta associated with the waking condition.

Vasishtha — The famous ancient rishi of India who was one of the mind-born sons of Lord Brahma, and who transmitted profound teachings to the Avatar, Sri Ram, when he was just a teenager.

Vedavyasa — Looked upon as "the Father of Vedanta," he collected many of the ancient scriptures of India upon the turning of an age, and thereby saved them from possible extinction.

Vichara — Inquiry into the nature of any aspect of Reality, such as the Atman, or a Mahavakya.

Vidhi — Rules and injunctions as stated in the scriptures.

Vidyashastra — Knowledge of the revealed scriptures; one of the three sources and proofs of spiritual life and realization.

Vijatiya-vrittis — Turbulent and contrary thoughts that arise in the mind, impeding meditation.

Vijnanamayakosha — The sheath of the intellect; the intellectual body as a covering over Reality.

Vikshepa — The distorting power of maya, also revealed through the distracting element of restlessness.

Vitarka — Debate; discussion; in Buddhism, doubts which arise that threaten to undermine one's balance and which, if unchecked, bring violent thoughts.

Vrittis — Mental vibrations, or waves; thought-forms.

Vyapakatma — The pervading quality of Absolute Consciousness and its Intelligent Particles.

Yoga — The overall practice of spirituality, which is also the goal of embodied beings seeking to realize Truth and Self.

Yukti — Adeptship in yoga; skillfulness; one of a succession of three practices by which the aspirant comes to realization. They are shruti, yukti and anubhava – studying the scriptures, reasoning about the truths therein and gaining direct spiritual experience.

SRV Associations of Oregon, San Francisco, & Hawaii

Other Books by Babaji Bob Kindler

- Twenty-Four Aspects of Mother Kali
    (Kindle edition e-book available)
- The Ten Divine Articles of Sri Durga
    (Kindle edition e-book available)
- The Avadhut and His Twenty-Four Teachers in Nature
- Sri Sarada Vijnanagita
- An Extensive Anthology of Sri Ramakrishna's Stories
- Swami Vivekananda Vijnanagita
- A Quintessential Yoga Vasishtha
- Reclaiming Kundalini Yoga
- Dissolving the Mindstream

Mini Series

- We Are Atman All-Abiding
- Strike Off Thy Fetters!
- Hasta-Amalaka Stotram

Planned Future Releases

- Footfalls of the Indian Rishis
- The Nine Limbs of Bhakti of Sri Ram
- Visions of the Goddess
- Guru Yoga in Contemporary Times
- White Crane, White Swan

Further inquiries at:
SRV Associations
P.O. Box 1364
Honoka'a, Hawaii 96727

website: www.srv.org
email: srvinfo@srv.org

www.ingramcontent.com/pod-product-compliance
Lightning Source LLC
Chambersburg PA
CBHW071004080526
44587CB00015B/2336